THE FILM ACTOR'S HANDBOOK

THE FILM ACTOR'S HANDBOOK

JESSE VINT

Copyright © 2010 by Jesse Vint

Published by Wolf's Eye Publishing

ISBN: 978-0-578-06564-9

All rights reserved. No part of this publication may be reproduced, stored in a retrieval system or transmitted, in any form, or by any means, electronic, mechanical, recorded, photocopied, or otherwise, without the prior written permission of both the copyright owner and the above publisher of this book, except by a reviewer who may quote brief passages in a review.

The scanning, uploading, and distribution of this book via the Internet or via any other means without the permission of the publisher is illegal and punishable by law. Please purchase only authorized electronic editions and do not participate on or encourage electronic piracy of copyrightable materials. Your support of the author's rights is appreciated.

Printed in the United States of America

Dedicated to

JLV4

CONTENTS

THE ABILITY TO MAKE PEOPLE CARE	9
WHAT REVOLUTION?	11
MAKING YOUR SCENE PARTNER THE MOST IMPORTANT PERSON IN THE ROOM	35
THE CONFLICT IN THE SCENE	38
CREATING A RELATIONSHIP WITH A HISTORY	41
USE OF AN EXISTING RELATIONSHIP	45
STREAMLINING YOUR APPROACH	56
LISTENING IS MANDATORY	62
THE PROBLEM OF ANTICIPATION	64
PRECONCEIVING THE SCENE	69
THE ULTIMATE HOT BUTTON	70
AN ACTOR'S RELAXATION	73
SKILL, TALENT, AND THE GOOD AMATEUR	77
A STRATEGY FOR THE EXTREMELY IMPORTANT, POTENTIALLY LIFE-ALTERING AUDITIONS	79
REHEARSALS	85
PREPARATION BEFORE THE DIRECTOR SAYS, "ACTION"	90
COMMON TRAPS FOR ACTORS	94
THE POTENTIAL TRAP WITHIN CHARACTER WORK	98

WORK WITH THE PLACE	103
RELATIONSHIP WITH THE CAMERA	107
CASTING DIRECTORS	115
DON'T BE DISCOURAGED BY CRANIAL DWARFISM	121
A MODEST WORD ABOUT FILM CRITICS	125
WHY ARE YOU GETTING PAID? (A Reminder)	127
THE WORLD'S MOST REWARDING BUSINESS	128

THE ABILITY TO MAKE PEOPLE CARE

LET'S get straight to it: If you're thinking about studying acting, then I'll have to ask you a question. It's a good question and goes straight to the core of all good acting.

"What's the difference between a good actor, and a star?"

The answer is that a good actor is believable, while a star has something beyond that—the star has the ability to make people care.

That's it. It sounds oversimplified—and maybe even preposterous to some, but if you can make an audience care about what is going on in the film, if you can make them worry about the outcome—then you're a star, and producers will seek you out and pay you exorbitant prices to do their film.

But before an actor can make people care, he must care himself. If the actor doesn't care, nobody else will care.

The final question then becomes:

"How does an actor make himself care about what is going on in a fictional screenplay with fictional relationships?"

The answer is—usually through a lot of hard work and study—but more simply, by knowing himself —or more specifically, *by knowing his hot buttons.*

Acting has been defined as a craft, a technique, and sometimes an art, but however you define it, there is no escaping the fact that it's a lot of hard work. We're not talking about just memorizing the lines. Memorizing the lines is usually about 5 percent of an actor's work. The other 95 percent is analysis of the script, character research, rehearsals, and most importantly, for an actor to know how to access his emotional life on cue.

I am definitely not speaking for all actors, nor would I, because finalized techniques vary with individual personalities. The Actor's Studio, Stanislavsky, and the method provide us with ideas to explore—a platform to proceed from and determine for ourselves what works for us as individuals—and what doesn't work. Although every individual finds his own way of getting there, the destination is pretty much the same for all actors—and that destination is *organic truth*. The other professional actors you work with (and even the audience) will easily detect falsified emotions. The simple truth is that there is no such thing as good acting without *internalizing*.

If an actor hasn't internalized his part then he has absolutely nothing. If you think that is an exaggeration then try this: Walk outside right now and drag in the first person that you see walking down the street. Regardless of who that person is, I can tell you that he has the ability to *pretend* to laugh, *pretend* to cry, and *pretend* to throw a tantrum, for *pretending* requires no talent whatsoever; it only requires a kind of shameless gall.

There are two types of actors in this world. There is the type of actor who *pretends to experience*, and then there's the type of actor who *actually experiences* on stage and in front of the camera. Since the revolution, discerning audiences now demand the latter.

WHAT REVOLUTION?

YEP, there was a revolution that started in Russia, and eventually engulfed the world. Here's what happened:

During the 1880's a young medical student put himself through medical school by writing short stories. His name was Anton Chekhov. By the time he graduated, he was famous throughout most of Russia as a short-story writer. Anton was born in 1860, so he achieved fame at an early age—during his mid-twenties. Years later Anton, totally enamored with the theatre, decided that he was going to write a play. He wrote a play called *The Seagull*. Although one of the main characters commits suicide offstage, Chekhov termed it a comedy. The play was staged and was a complete disaster. Chekhov vowed to stick with his short stories and to never write another play.

A brilliant young director named Constantin Stanislavsky, who was three years younger than Chekhov, and like everyone else a great admirer of his short stories, contacted him and invited him to a rehearsal of *The Seagull*, saying that they thought the play had great potential. The word is that Chekhov recoiled at the idea, not wanting to be disgraced again by his playwriting effort, but in the end agreed to sit through a rehearsal at the Moscow Art Theatre.

At the end of the run-through Stanislavski turned to Chekhov and asked, "Well, what do you think?"

Chekhov thought for a while, and then said this one sentence that set Constantin Stanislavsky and the Moscow Art Theatre on a course that would in time become revolutionary. Chekhov simply said: "I would like it a lot better if the actors didn't act so much." Quintessential Chekhov. If "Brevity is the soul of wit," as Shakespeare said, then Chekhov was a very witty man.

After Chekhov left the theatre that day, Stanislavsky began to ask himself, "But why should actors act at all?" He probably wondered why actors can't be the same as the people in Chekhov's short stories, who were full of doubt, socially awkward, blushing, self-conscious, always feeling out of place, striving to be included, and continually struggling to make sense out of their lives. Why does there have to be strutting, bellowing extroverts whose chief effort is to shamelessly draw attention to themselves—as some actors did then, and are still doing to this day? It apparently was a problem for Chekhov, just as it was with Shakespeare. Prince Hamlet goes on for three pages about this very subject when he hires his acting troupe to perform in the castle to expose the villainy of his uncle. According to the prince, the play must be performed realistically, and the actors were told in no uncertain terms that they were "To hold, as it t'were, the mirror up to nature …"

Of course this is Shakespeare telling his actors, now and forever, that he was completely fed up with strutting, bellowing, actors destroying his plays. He very explicitly and unequivocally laid out a roadmap for his actors, saying "I would have a fellow whipped for o'erdoing Termagant. It out-Herods Herod. Pray you avoid it."

And in another unambiguous admonishment, he said "Oh

there be players that I have heard play, and heard others praise, and that highly; not to speak it profanely, but having neither the accent of Christians, nor the gait of Christians, nor pagan, nor man, have so strutted and bellowed that I thought some of nature's journeymen had made men, and not made them well, they imitated humanity so abominably. Pray you avoid it!"

After *Hamlet* (registered in 1601) Shakespeare left no doubt in anybody's mind that he wanted his actors to "O'erstep not the modesty of nature ..." while performing his plays.

After Chekhov left the theatre that day The Moscow Art Theatre began an experiment in acting that was the very beginning of the revolution. The actors actually lived on stage; they fed their cats and dogs on stage, cooked their meals, took a bath, napped, read the newspaper, so that when they began their dialogue there were no discernible differences in their demeanor. They took their characters into the streets for flight tests and learned to function wholly and truthfully as the characters they were playing. If they were caught acting by the locals on the street, then they had failed in their mission. It was genuine artistic dedication.

For the audiences who were first witnessing this new approach, it was not as though the curtain were being raised so much, as it was a fourth wall being removed. The audience's experience was entirely unique. Chekhov's *The Sea Gull* was a hit, and soon the Stanislavsky revolution moved westward.

Anton Chekhov 1860–1904

Anton Chekhov was very much encouraged after that, and wrote several more plays that became classical theatre before dying of tuberculosis at the impossibly young age of forty-four in 1904.

I'm probably the only one who thinks this, but Chekhov's plays will never be as good as his short stories—for this reason: When Chekhov writes a story, basically, through his narrative description, you are given a tour of the place and its people by one of the greatest literary minds that have ever lived. His narration, description of the town, landscape, people, events, and situations is so incredibly unique that it can only be described as "Chekhovian." There is no other word to accurately describe Chekhov's style.

Ernest Hemmingway once said that "All writers start out imitating Anton Chekhov until they find their own style."

Now, when you watch one of his plays, you see the characters, the situations, and you hear the dialogue—but what you don't get is Chekhov as the most insightful friend you've ever had walking through the town with you describing everything and everybody in ways that are unimaginably humorous and brilliant. But still, his plays are now, and always will be great theatre. As far as modern theatre goes, Chekhov, to me, is second only to Ibsen—but that's just me. The greatest modern play of them all, I believe, is Ibsen's *Enemy of the People*. That play ferrets out a tragic truth about the human race that will unfortunately probably always exist. It's a plot has been used in many popular films, including *Jaws*.

In the early 1920s Stanislavsky came to America and the Moscow Art theatre performed for New Yorkers in the Russian language. This made a huge impact on New York's theatrical community, and in the 1930s a theatrical entity known as "The Group Theatre" came into being and experimented with "the Stanislavsky method." It successfully staged many Marxist-themed plays during the thirties, and then crumbled to pieces around 1940. The various members then formed their individual acting schools, each claiming to be a direct disciple of Stanislavsky, and strangely enough (or maybe not) began jockeying for position and rivaling one another. In fact, they bad-mouthed one another non-stop. I studied with both Strasberg and Adler, and they never let up on each other. But the names of these instructors are well known, even today. Some of the names were Stella Adler, Lee Strasberg, Sanford Meisner, Harold Clurman, Bobby Lewis, Cheryl Crawford, and perhaps the greatest of them all, director Elia Kazan.

At this point the Stanislavsky system remained an esoteric New York buzzword, until one day a nineteen-year-old-kid wandered out of a cornfield in Nebraska—straight off a working farm. The kid went to New York City to visit his sister, Jocelyn Brando. While there he amazed his sister and her friends with his impressions of various New Yorkers. Marlon, no doubt, saw this as the greatest people-watching fest of his life. Being from Oklahoma and landing by Greyhound bus in New York City, I know exactly what this was about. I saw a greater variety of human beings from various cultures in New York City in the first two hours than in all my Oklahoma years combined. It was nothing less than astonishing. It had to be in some ways similar for the kid from Nebraska.

The entire story is far and away better told in Marlon Brando's terrific book *Brando on Brando*. Please read it. But also know that he is modest in this book and would personally cringe at being called "the revolutionary." But here's what Jack Nicholson said at Brando's funeral:

> Marlon Brando was the beginning and the end of his own revolution. There was no following in his footsteps. He was just too large, and too far out of sight.

Admirably said by the world's most-loved actor. I have to say that when Jack Nicholson is dead serious, he is the funniest person I have ever been around. I spent three days on *Chinatown* early in my career apologizing to him for laughing uncontrollably when he was telling me and Roman Polanski something that he was dead serious about ("We're in the midst of an alien takeover …"). But the whole thing was one of my all-time favorite experiences.

At the very young age of twenty-three, Marlon Brando opened on Broadway with the Tennessee Williams play *Streetcar Named Desire* in 1947 directed by the great Elia Kazan. After that the world of acting was never the same. It was the first time that anybody had truly exemplified the Stanislavsky method, as it came to be called. The play was packed every single night, because people—mostly actors—were seeing it over and over again, trying to figure out just what in the hell this guy was doing. He wasn't acting, it seemed. Soon the debates were raging in the New York City coffee shops newspapers, and magazines.

"How can you say that this guy is a good actor—when he's not acting? That's just who he is. He's like that. He actually is like Stanley Kowalski. I've met him. I know. So how is he acting, already?"

These doubters were soon to eat their words. Brando was cast as Marc Anthony in Shakespeare's *Julius Caesar*. The Brits were not happy about this. This was an American kid out of a Nebraska cornfield who had never done a Shakespearean play in his life and was probably, they felt, being cast in this part only so that the film's investors had a way of protecting their investment by including the American film-going market.

"It's wrong! We've got thousands of actors all over the island who have been doing Shakespeare since age ten." they said. From what I understand, he received a harsh welcome.

One week into the shooting they realized that acting history was being made. By the end of the film everybody wanted to be his best friend. Soon many of the British greats were saying that their favorite actor was Marlon Brando. Brando did not disappoint. The following year, 1954, he won a best actor Oscar for his legendary performance in *On the Waterfront*.

Marlon Brando as Marc Anthony in the film *Julius Caesar*.

Brando's performance as Marc Anthony is still, to this day, my favorite performance by any actor. The degree of difficulty for this Shakespearean play and character, particularly for someone who had never done Shakespeare, was a ten. In this movie you can watch for yourself, like no other movie ever made, the two different schools of acting within the same movie. It is in some ways hilarious. Not to speak it profanely, but most of the Brits looked like actors wandering around in their bathrobes after having just told their fellow actors a joke while eating a donut—and then were tapped on the shoulder and told that they were up.

And then came Brando, looking like a marble statue of a Roman patrician being pushed towards the camera, and then suddenly coming to life, his eyes burning with rage, his soul on fire, when he viewed the body of his good friend and mentor, Julius Caesar, who had been stabbed twenty-three times by nineteen of his fellow senators.

Yet Marc Anthony was in a predicament. If he showed too

much loyalty to Caesar, they would take him down. If he showed too little, than he was a disloyal sycophant, a political prostitute whose soul conformed to the corkscrew political machinations of the moment—like most politicians. It was a tightrope that Marc Anthony walked. Brando threaded that needle brilliantly—like no other actor in the world. As he reluctantly shook each one of the assassin's hands, you could hear the *history of the relationship* that Marc Anthony had with each character he spoke to. And then, of course, the masterful way he turned the crowd against Brutus would have, I have no doubt, made Shakespeare weep with joy, grateful that an actor had finally internalized one of his characters, and had "held the mirror up to nature."

It's called *the method* by some, *internalizing* by others, and *organic truth* by most, but whatever you call it— it gained prominence almost overnight because of Marlon Brando.

The debates about Brando came to a screeching halt. Nobody could accuse him of actually being like the Roman patrician Marc Anthony in life—and then asking, "So where's the challenge?" Most of the doubters became supporters. Everybody across the country, and from overseas, flocked to Stella Adler and the Actor's Studio to find the Brando magic.

Then another guy walked out of a cornfield from a working farm—this time in Indiana. His name was James Dean. Both Marlon Brando and James Dean shared a very, very unique ability:

Both of these farm boys, Dean and Brando, had the ability to transport an audience member to another time and space almost immediately—and keep them there, long after the film was over.

These two actually went beyond "making an audience care," for they inhabited the mind and soul of the American youth, generating a cultural revolution in the fifties that was to cascade and spread to all other art forms throughout the world.

They were straight out of the American cornfields, and that's something that bewildered New Yorkers to no end—at least when I was there.

The Indiana farm where James Dean was raised

James Dean was killed in a Porsche Spyder 30 Sept 1955 at age twenty-four after just three films. I believe that James Dean would have eventually performed Hamlet, and like Brando with Marc Anthony, turned in a legendary performance that would have shut the door on all other "Prince Hamlet" attempts.

At the time of this writing there is only one living expert on how James Dean worked as an actor, and that is the extraordinarily gifted Martin Landau, whose is currently the executive director of the Actor's Studio West. Martin Landau was a good friend of James Dean.

Elia Kazan had founded the Actor's Studio, and appointed Lee Strasberg to administer it while he was out of town directing films with Brando and Dean. That alone is the official tie-in to the legends of Brando and Dean to the Actor's Studio. The irony is that neither actor actually studied there. Brando studied with Stanislavsky disciple Stella Adler, and Dean studied at various places for short periods of time, and it's true that both attended sessions at the Actor's Studio. But both were definitely students of Elia Kazan while working on his films, and Elia Kazan was the founder of the Actor's Studio—he was the mentor's mentor. He utilized the principles of Stanislavsky like no other and was without a doubt the greatest *organic* film director of all time.

STEP I: WHEN HANDED A SCRIPT WHAT DO YOU DO?

The first thing you do when handed a script, of course, is to read it and re-read it. Some actors read the script over many, many times, gleaning something useful each time.

The script is a blueprint—it's a clue to the reality—it is a means of finding the life below the words—more commonly known as the "subtext." You have to do some detective work, but finding the subtext is an essential part of an actor's work.

To begin this search, ask yourself this question:

(a) "What is my character's problem?"

Sometimes it's easy. If the script says that your son has been kidnapped, then there is no mystery at all; but if it's about four sisters getting together at their mother's house in Michigan to sort things out after their mother's death, then you're dealing with all kinds of various motives and psychological complexities that go back to their early childhoods. It may take several rehearsals before the character's problem becomes perfectly clear—but it must be made clear. Clarity is essential.

Once the character's problem is clear, then it is very helpful, I have found, to make a segue from a *problem* to a *predicament*:

(b) "What is my character's predicament?"

What predicament is your character in that he or she has to get out of?

Here's why this is very helpful: You can take a non-actor, somebody who has never even thought about acting, and put that person into an improvisational *situation*—better yet, a *predicament*—and if that person has **absolute clarity** *about the predicament, he or she* can do surprisingly well— without a single minute of formal training.

For example, consider telling a seventeen-year-old teen-ager who has never studied acting in her life that her parents are saying goodbye as they go to the lake for the weekend, leaving her with explicit instructions to not have a single house guest over for any reason. The teenager agrees to this, and once the parents drive away, the teenage girl immediately texts her boyfriend and tells him that the coast is clear. The boyfriend comes right over and then suddenly without warning the parents return, because they forgot something ....

Let's just say that the boyfriend is stuffed into a closet as the parents walk through the door to retrieve whatever it is that they forgot—and then they notice something unusual. They began to linger and snoop around ....

The teenage girl is in a *predicament*, and her mind and body are no longer on cruise control. Now her mind, heart, body, and soul are united for a common pursuit—an *intention* (as we called it at the Actor's Studio), an *objective* (as Stanislavsky calls it) or a *mission*, as I like to call it. The teenage girl's entire being is brainstorming for a solution on how to get out of this predicament.

When breaking down a script, look for the predicament that the character is in. If you can improvise on this predicament, sometimes using your own lines—and sometimes using lines from the script, then your chances of soaring are far better. The bottom line is that the first thing you do with the script is to find the problem/predicament that your character is in. Once you begin to feel *the push and pull of the predicament*, then you are positioned to fly. The mission will then come naturally. In this case the young girl's mission would probably be *to distract her parents* so that they don't open the closet. She might take them out into the backyard, or into the garage, citing strange noises or whatever, while the boyfriend makes his escape.

The words will be there to assist you in fulfilling your mission—as they should be. But the words are not the reality—they are only a clue to the reality.

The words are the writer's contribution to the film. The actor's contribution is to bring heart and soul to those words.

(c) On a mission.

Escaping the predicament becomes a *mission* that the actor goes on. Once the actor is on a mission that unites mind body and soul, then that actor begins to function, not at the 5 percent we normally function at in everyday life, but at the 95 percent that a good predicament/crisis normally demands.

A really good script always puts the actor in some kind of *situation/predicament/crisis* that demands his finest resources to get out of. You see this from scene to scene to scene as you watch a movie, and this is a big part of what gives an actor his higher-than-life quality on screen—he is usually at the 95 percent crisis level—and almost never on cruise control—even in comedy.

An actor who is caught in a predicament is given the opportunity to use his resources, known as his personality, temperament, natural persuasiveness, intelligence, presence, physicality, imagination—or all of these combined to escape the predicament. Ultimately, for me, how well he does this is an important measure of his strength as an actor. It's not the only measure, but it's definitely a measure. His ability *to make people care* is inextricably bound to these resources.

The force of an actor's personality then becomes an essential ingredient. It's important. When they cast DiCaprio in *Revolutionary Road,* they have to cast a strong personality opposite him to make the film fly. Here's why:

If you were watching The Superbowl and the score at half-time was 56 to 0, what would happen? The spectators, of course, would get up and leave and walk to their cars to beat the traffic. There's no more suspense. There is no war. It's all over. The outcome is already certain.

It's the same in movies. The teams must be strong and evenly matched to have a good film play right to the end. That's why you need a Kate Winslett opposite DiCaprio. Not just any actress will do.

In *Casino* you need a strong confrontational actress like Sharon Stone, with multiple resources to go toe to toe with the likes of Robert De Niro. Not just any famous, talented beautiful blonde will do. An ordinary actress would be flattened by the strength of Robert De Niro. There would be no movie—and the audience would leave at half-time.

Joe Pesci is frequently cast opposite De Niro for the same reason. He is small, but dynamic. As everybody knows by now, he is a very strong, forceful, and persuasive personality.

The very first time I saw Joe Pesci was in the classic *Raging Bull*, and I was astonished that this actor, who I had never seen before, was going toe to toe with De Niro and holding his own. But if you met Joe Pesci in a restaurant (and I have), and didn't know who he was, you would never guess that he had this kind of confrontational strength. Unless it's John Wayne (Shaking hands with him was like shaking hands with the Grand Canyon.), you usually cannot tell an actor's strength by looking at him. Some seem to, on sight, have a physical gift, but it's truly nothing until that actor is on a mission against another actor who is also on a mission *that is exactly the opposite in purpose*. Then you'll start to see what that actor is about, and what use he has, if any, to the film industry.

As a final word on this, Darth Vader goes up against Luke Skywalker, Dr. No goes up against James Bond, the medieval dragon goes up against the brave knight, Shane goes up against Jack Wilson, and on and on. It doesn't make storytelling sense to have a weakling who is easily overpowered go up against someone that is strong, powerful, and dominant. There is no tension when one side is easily flattened. It is one of the chief reasons why casting is so important.

SUMMARY

1. First read the script several times, focusing on every aspect of the script just as intently as you focus on the part that you are playing.
2. Ask yourself, "What is my character's problem?"
3. Refine that a little bit and ask, "What *predicament* am I in?" (I am now speaking in the first person. Some people choose to do that—while others prefer to say "my character.")
4. Ask yourself, "How am I going to get out of this predicament?" The answer to that question is your "mission." The actor who comes through the doorway with an agenda, an intention, an objective, *a mission* that is deeply *internalized* is an actor who is immediately captivating. An actor who wanders about without purpose is one you probably won't see much of—because he didn't get the part. He was eliminated by actors who are on a mission and have *internalized* that mission. The difference between the two actors is so blatant that a trained eye is not necessary to distinguish between them.

STEP II: MOVING THE INFORMATION FROM HEAD TO HEART

The writer of a screenplay or novel probably could probably analyze the material better than anybody else. Tennessee Williams could more than likely give you a detailed psychological profile and history of his main characters that is second to no one; but Tennessee Williams could not act these parts—for this reason: He doesn't know how to move the information from his head to his heart and fire it on cue. He doesn't know how to "get out of his head," as the problem is sometimes defined.

It's an actor's job to move that information from his head to his heart, and regardless of how many rehearsals he's had, to make it look like it's occurring for the first time. This step is the hard part. It's what separates the actor's art from all other arts. It's not an easy thing to do.

(a) Knowing Your Hot Buttons

To move this information from head to heart and rise to the crisis level that most screenplays demand, an actor must know who he is; he must know his *hot buttons*. He must know what creates a meltdown, a road-rage incident, throwing a cell phone, punching somebody out, crying uncontrollably, laughing hysterically, the pain of heartbreak, the joy of a pure love, the outrage of betrayal, the excruciating fear of having a loved one in extreme danger, love at first sight, the inconsolable grief of losing a loved one, and on and on. A movie is not everyday life; it's a two-hour compression of highly intense experiences.

These hot buttons are warehoused in a huge storage area known as the subconscious. When an actor actively utilizes these hot buttons in his work, it is known as *internalizing*. As an actor you can speak with an accent, walk with a limp, wear a false nose, laugh, cry, have a meltdown, but it means absolutely nothing unless it's internalized.

Stanislavsky devoted his long life to the clinical examination of actors and what brings them to life on stage. He felt that the reason actors very often seem so incomplete as human beings on stage is that their subconscious is never really activated. The reason for this is that some actors believe that they can go directly to the result by making direct demands on their emotional life. The amateur believes that he can order his soul to be happy, be sad, be angry, be joyful, be sexually turned on, be full of rage, or have a meltdown by simply willing it. This is known by professionals as going directly to the result, or more simply as "result acting." Result acting is almost always 100 percent fraudulent.

When people laugh, cry, blush, or fly into a rage, these are *involuntary* emotions. These things happen as a result of something else—a precondition. It is the actor's job to find out what that "something else" is. I call them "hot buttons." These hot buttons are lurking around in every human being, some more so than others, and some are more easily detonated than others.

The *involuntary emotional life* that is consistent with the character is the actor's quest. When an actor struggles not to laugh, the audience will struggle with him. When an actor struggles not to cry, the audience will struggle with this also. The best example that I can think of is Jack Nicholson in the terrific film *Five Easy Pieces*. Nicholson said in an interview afterwards that he was actually supposed to cry in another part of the film, but something overtook him in that scene with his father, who had had a stroke and was now confined to his wheelchair. It's one of the most moving scenes in cinema. It's entirely involuntary, and it gets many of us every time—even when we know it's coming. This is what Stanislavsky, Shakespeare, and Anton Chekhov had in mind when they were telling the actors in so many words to "stop acting."

(b) Locating Your Hot Buttons

This is an actor's homework, but I can give the actor a couple of questions that will help him find those hot buttons. They are very personal, and no instructor should intrude on an actor's privacy by asking him what these hot buttons represent. But here's a suggestion on how to find a couple:

1. What is the best phone call that you could get?

2. What is the worst phone call that you could get?

In most cases the answers that you give are your reasons for getting out bed in the morning. These answers define what's important to you; they, in many ways, are the engine that drives you throughout the day. To incorporate these things into your work as an actor is your job. That is what you get paid for.

Just as these things are the engine that drives you throughout your day, these same things will be the engine that drives you through a script. They will give you the power that you need when you go toe to toe with a strong personality.

It's vitally important to know these hot buttons and how to use them in your work.

Here is a great example: There was an actor in my class who studied with me for about six months. This particular actor, about twenty-two years old, was a propped-up cadaver. He had been studying the Meisner technique with various Meisnerites in Portland for several years when he came to me. His routine was to set up a romantic scene with an attractive lady, bore everyone to tears, and then turn to the class and wait for the verdict.

This particular scene was about an intensely romantic relationship with a woman he was living with. This woman, according to the script, was the woman of his dreams, and he was madly in love with her. But when she finally walked out the door for good at the end of the scene, there was nothing that indicated this Meisnerite cared for her in the slightest. Even then, he didn't appear to have a pulse. I started out by asking:

"Have you ever been in love?"

"Nope!"

"Have you ever had a soul mate, anybody that you really cared about, anybody at all?"

"Nope!"

"Why in God's name did you choose this scene?"

"I consider it a challenge," he shrugged.

"Well, since caring about another person in a romantic sense seems to be totally outside your experience, this scene would definitely be a challenge for you. How did you go about working on this scene?"

"I just let it flow."

"In order to let something flow, there first must be something there—that's contained. What exactly did you let flow?"

"I don't get into that; it's too analytical. I'm a Meisner guy." (He actually said this, word for word.)

"Okay. What is the worst phone call that you could get? You don't have to tell me if you don't want to." (He thought for the count of ten.)

"I don't mind. The worst thing that could happen to me is that my race car is stolen out of my garage."

"Okay. What's the best phone call that you could get?" (He thought for the count of five.)

"That my sponsor wants to renew my racing contract for another year."

At this point it was clear to me that he had no room for anyone in his life—not even a cat, a dog, a goldfish, or a plant, because he was so obsessed by his race car. His race car encompassed his past, present, and future, and all that was valuable and worthwhile in his life. His race car was his hot button—his only hot button. Now, the job for me was to hot-wire his scene partner to that race car—so that they were inextricably bound to one another. I called him outside the class and said to him:

"Here's the deal. That girl has inherited 1.2 million dollars. She owns the race car. She *is* your sponsor. Now think about this, and allow yourself to gently drift into this zone without forcing anything at all. Let the scene come to you—and try to remember what life will be like when she walks out that door. Your life will be empty, dead, without a single ray of sunshine, and you will find yourself on the shady side of an iceberg forever, with no four-wheel drifts to dream about, no checkered flags, no straight-pipe thunder on all sides of you as you snake through the pack, (The cadaver's face began to show some color.) no screaming crowds jumping to their feet and yelling your name ... there will be nothing ... nothing but a vast eternal darkness where you will be left alone to weep and to gnash your teeth in bitter despair."

"Christ Almighty! How did you know all of this about racing?"

"I raced at Ascot Park for over a year in '71 with the Mears brothers. Now go out there and make sure that she does not get through that door—no matter what—otherwise your race car is gone with the wind. But you cannot stop her through physical force—that's where you draw the line. Got it?"

By this time he was trembling, while his eyes danced in his head.

"I got it!"

The scene began. You should have seen how the cadaver came to life, hurling himself in front of her, blocking the doorway—and then how he dropped to his knees and tackled her around the waist, while wailing and sobbing away.

He violated the mandate I gave him to not stop her with physical force, but I let it go because, for the first time as an actor, he was beside himself with a fear of loss.

The situation was clear to him; He was in a predicament. His life was about to be overturned and devastated by the loss of his race car—and *he was on a mission* to make sure that that didn't happen. He had successfully detonated his only hot button, and it was highly explosive.

In one way I thought it was one of the most interesting things I had ever seen, and in another way I thought that I was witnessing something dark and terrible. I recalled Hamlet's words after he asked an actor to perform a piece from a Greek play, and as the actor did so these thoughts involuntarily crept into Hamlet's head:

> *Is it not monstrous that this player here,*
> *But in a fiction, in a dream of passion,*
> *Could force his soul so to his own conceit*
> *That from her working all his visage wann'd,*
> *Tears in his eyes, distraction in's aspect,*
> *A broken voice, and his whole function suiting*
> *With forms to his conceit? and all for nothing!*
> *For Hecuba!*
> *What's Hecuba to him, or he to Hecuba,*
> *That he should weep for her?*

Hecuba owned his race car and was about to take it away—that's what Hecuba was to him. The cadaver was suddenly brought to life, and I felt a little like Dr. Frankenstein.

The audience gave the two actors a robust applause. Some of them even stood up while applauding. The young actor called me three days later and told me he was leaving for Los Angeles to try his luck, that he understood acting now, he knew how to internalize, that studying with the Meisnerites for years was a colossal waste of time and money, he now knew the secret of the art of acting, and he wondered whether I had any advice.

I advised him not to sell his race car—without elaborating. As it turned out he understood, for he solemnly said these words: "I'll never sell my race car. That race car is my soul; it's who I am—it's what I'm about."

He was exactly right. His race car was the engine that drove his life. He didn't own his race car—it owned him. It's good that he finally knew this, but it's far more important that he knew how to use this in his work as an actor.

A really good actor knows how to load up the script with his hot buttons. He has learned who he is, and which of his hot buttons fire with what percentage of reliability. He knows this because he has taken the time to record these moments during his study. He knows the exact preconditions to the explosion, or the meltdown. Once a good actor has hard-wired these hot buttons to his mission, the script then looks to him like a minefield. Remember:

Never get caught acting. It'll ruin your career as an actor.

MAKING YOUR SCENE PARTNER THE MOST IMPORTANT PERSON IN THE ROOM

I have already given you one example of this—the actor who cared only about his race car. Once he saw that his scene partner was the sole benefactor of his racing career, she became the most interesting person in the room, to say the least.

There are other ways to do this. It's very common in an acting class (and even with professionals) to watch two people try to connect who have absolutely no interest in one another. The effort then becomes forced. The key is to know what gets people out of bed in the morning. If you have an actress who cares about nothing in life except fame and fortune, then if she suddenly imagined her scene partner, physically unattractive and boring as he may be, to be a writer for Time magazine that is doing a cover story about "*The struggle of up and coming actresses in America,*" then he will suddenly, to her, take on a charm and gallantry that never existed prior to that knowledge. She will began to find his words fascinating, his manner totally captivating, and his pop n' fresh doughboy physical appearance is somehow magically transformed into that of a roguish devil-may-care swashbuckler. He effortlessly becomes the most important person in the room, for nobody in the room can do more for her life than this single individual—not the producer, director, or the audience. Her innate resources no longer slumber in the presence of "Pop n' Fresh," but are involuntarily called forth, and she becomes, without effort, as interesting as she can possibly be. Regardless of what the scene is about, in most cases she becomes fun to watch. She has activated her soul.

Know yourself, your ultimate goals, and what activates your soul—that is always the key.

I read where Sanford Meisner once said that there are only two motives in life—sex and money. If that were true then there would be no such thing as charities, adrenalin adventures, love for wildlife and the great outdoors, family relationships, and love at first sight—to mention a few. I doubt that he said that—but if he did, he must have been one miserable codger.

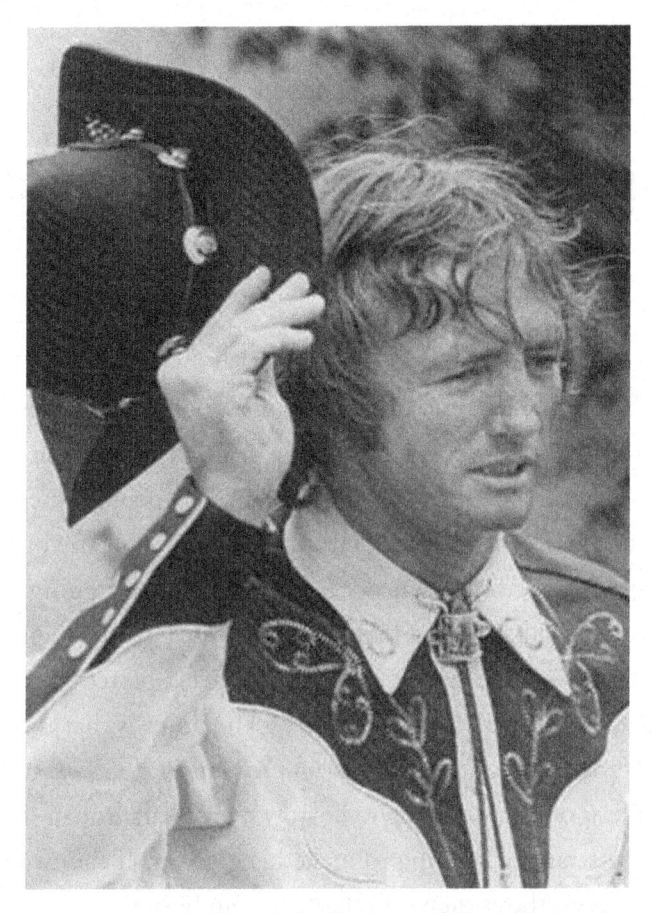

As "Slick Callahan" in *Bobby Jo and the Outlaw*

THE CONFLICT IN THE SCENE

THE actor being on a mission against another actor who is on an exact opposite mission is the "conflict within the scene." There is always a conflict, for this reason: Two people agreeing on everything is a chat scene at Starbuck's. How long can you watch that—twenty seconds? But once the people start arguing, everybody turns their heads to look. If a fight breaks out, then it gets real exciting—some people stand up to get a better look, while others makes a break for the doorway. The point is that the writer always provides the actors with a *conflict within the scene*. It can be as simple as one actor trying to borrow five dollars from a stranger, while the stranger is trying to make his getaway. If the two actors agree on everything then everybody can go home.

The actors are almost always at cross purposes with each other. *Acting is doing,* so you must be clear about what your character is doing in the scene. One way to find out is to ask yourself the question, "Why don't I just get up and leave now?" You will find yourself saying, "Because I have unfinished business," and then it is usually much easier to define just exactly what that unfinished business is.

Another way is to ask yourself, "What is the other character trying to do?" You are probably trying to do the opposite;

otherwise there would be no scene. Again, a scene is almost always a scene because two people are disagreeing about something.

A good script very often traps characters in an urgent situation—and they try to escape.

If it's drama, things often can be summed up in one word—*danger!* If it's comedy, things often can again be summed up in one word—*embarrassment!*

That may sound over-simplified to some, just as "E=MC squared" sounds oversimplified, but it's really not. Complex problems can be reduced down to simple equations. Mark Twain reduced the source of all comedy to a single factor—human misery. He's probably right. Next time that you watch a comedy, observe this for yourself. The character is probably miserable from some kind of deep embarrassment—and that's why an actor can never be in the same frame of mind as the audience:

An actor and his audience are never in the same space.

An audience member suffers his pain and misery when he plops down twenty dollars for he and his date—and then another twenty for popcorn and drinks, so he's in forty to fifty dollars by the time the movie begins.

Now it's the actor's turn to suffer pain—whether it's comedy or drama. He is now probably running from gunshots in a drama, or dying of embarrassment in a comedy, but whatever it is that he is doing, he is most certainly not drinking a coke and eating popcorn with a smile on his face. The actor's mind should *never* travel out into the audience and take a seat. With amateurs, the temptation to do this is as natural as a horse's desire to run back to the barn. They tend to watch themselves. It's a natural desire that has to be tamed.

Actors are required to reach down inside themselves for these emotional experiences, and that's sometimes difficult. Many of these painful experiences are locked up for a reason, and it's not always easy to open these doors. But that's an actor's job. That's what he does. He can't fly under the radar by simply pretending to experience these things. Those days, among the top pros at least, are long gone.

The movie usually promises a showdown between light and dark, good and evil, wrong and right. The story is usually moving toward that conclusion, and it is the promise of that showdown that keeps the audience members glued to their seats.

As mentioned previously, a strong, confrontational, and persuasive personality will certainly help an actor fight for his cause when the showdown begins; and in a good film there is always a cause. Sometimes the cause is representing the working class, a civil rights issue, or "Joan of Ark" rallying the French to defend against the English—or "Terry Malloy" (Brando in *On the Waterfront*) fighting deeply-entrenched corruption within the gangster-ridden labor unions. To rise to these uber-levels that are far more intense than the levels found in normal daily life, it's mandatory to know your hot buttons. Your hot buttons provide the rocket-fuel that gives you the confrontational strength that you need to represent a class, a group of people, or even a nation—just as adrenalin is necessary for an Olympic athlete to cross the finish line first. Without it that athlete doesn't have a chance of winning.

(More about hot buttons later)

CREATING A RELATIONSHIP WITH A HISTORY

IN most cases you don't have an existing relationship with your fellow actors. They are usually strangers who show up and introduce themselves to one another. The relationships in the script have to be created. There are very specific ways to do this.

When you are interacting with another character in a play, you have to know what the *history of that relationship* is. Whether it's your mother, stepmother, father, brother, best friend, or soul mate, you have a unique history with that person, and it has to be thought about and defined before you can proceed with any real accuracy.

In any relationship you have things that are okay to say and do, and things that are not okay to say and do. It's a paperless contract with one another. Most of the time formal lines have been declared, and these lines are not to be crossed, or it creates a rupture in the relationship—and a war breaks out. The purpose of that war is either to enforce the existing boundaries, or redraw new ones.

It is exactly the same with countries. A river serves as a boundary between two countries. The river floods, and when the flood recedes the two countries discover that the river has changed its course, redefining the boundaries to some, but not to others. A dispute breaks out between north and south about where the true boundaries lie. It cannot be solved by dialogue, so the two countries go to war. It's a volatile chapter, and a lot of people die.

People go to war with each other for exactly the same reasons—because boundaries were crossed that were formerly agreed upon. It becomes volatile, and sometimes people will die. So knowing the history of the relationship and where the lines are drawn is essential.

Your relationship with one brother might be entirely different than your relationship with another brother. One borrows money constantly with absolutely no intention of paying it back, and the other brother's nature is exactly the opposite. One brother could be a pathological liar, and the other brother never lies about anything. When you say even one word to the two different brothers, such as, "Hello," the difference, or the *history of the relationship* should be discernible—even to an untrained ear.

When you show up on a movie set you will very often meet the other actors for the first time. They introduce this one as your mother, and that one as your best friend, another one as your girlfriend, and another as your worst enemy. None of these relationships actually exist. They have to be created from scratch.

But how?

Actors usually begin by identifying elements of another person with whom they have a history. They focus on those familiar aspects that are consistent with their vision of the character playing opposite them. For example, if you have a scene with an actor whose character is an attorney—and that attorney is written as a well-known lying, deceptive fraud who can never be counted on to tell the truth—and you have had an experience with such an attorney, then your job is a little easier. The next step is to find similar elements in the actor who is playing that attorney. It might be the actor's physicality, or it could be elements of his or her personality that are consistent with the attorney with whom you have a history—or sometimes it's both. If this is the case, then write down the similarities so that your work will be *specific,* and you don't lose sight of what you're trying to accomplish. Remember Stanislavsky's words when he said: *In general is the enemy of art!* Always be specific.

As "Bob Dalton" in *Belle Starr*

Your work with the other actor, then, is to graft those similarities from the real attorney with whom you have a history onto the actor that you have just met—so that you organically respond in a like manner. Once you begin the rehearsal, focus on these similarities between the real attorney and the person playing the attorney, being careful not to force responses to conform to an idea. After a couple of run-throughs, you should be able to tell whether this is working for you.

It is in this manner that you can create separate and specific relationships with every member of the cast, until neutral bystanders are absolutely convinced that you have a history outside the workplace with one another.

At the Actor's Studio, we called this utilization of people from your past *personalizing*. Personalizing then, is creating a history with a complete stranger. The way to tell whether the personalization is working is if your responses come *effortlessly* in a manner consistent with the demands of the script.

"Effortlessly" is a huge word, and usually describes the very finest in any chosen profession. If you notice, whether it's a golfer, a boxer, or a snow skier—when they are truly on their game they look effortless. With the novice you see the *torture of the effort*, and that's about all you see. The pro makes it look easy.

There's an old Chinese proverb that truly applies to acting:

Try hard, but not too hard.

James Dean, Marlon Brando, and even John Wayne made acting look so easy that everybody thought they too could do it—and they left their homes for Hollywood by the thousands every year. But if it were easy, then everybody would be doing it—and on some of those auditions I was out on, I was convinced that everybody *was* doing it.

USE OF AN EXISTING RELATIONSHIP

I registered for an audition at the Actor's Studio within a few days of arriving in Los Angeles. The problem for me, though, was that I didn't know a soul in the state of California. I had no scene partner to audition with. Then my brother Alan showed up on a motorcycle. He had ridden five hundred miles from the University of Arizona where he was studying engineering to say hello and meet the girl I had married. We were having coffee with Stephanie when it occurred to me to ask him to audition with me; so I did. I told him that we could do the scene between two brothers in *Death of a Salesman*. He had never studied acting, or even thought about it, so he thought that I was hallucinating. I argued the point, though, that as brothers in real life we had a huge warehouse of common information that we could tap into—and that if we just stayed with the brother relationship, and didn't try to interpret the material for them, which I was sure they didn't care about anyway, then we could very possibly do something unique. I also told him that they probably didn't care about him anyway since it was my audition. That seemed to take some pressure off. He reluctantly agreed. He figured that this venture, though bound to be embarrassing, would be an anonymous embarrassment, because he would soon be on his motorcycle headed back to Arizona.

We drew on each other's history throughout the audition, and for the most part never tried to make sense out of anything. When I said, "I think Dad's going crazy ..." He started laughing, and when Alan laughs, his laugh soon morphs into something that sounds like a donkey braying with multiple squeals on the intake. This has always caused me to laugh. We both were laughing in all the wrong places, and somber in all the wrong places. It was all wrong—all of it—except that we were "two totally organic guys that could not hit a false note if we tried"—as the judges said later of us. One of them also said that we were "so wrong, that we were right." I liked that description best of all.

Alan never returned to Arizona to study engineering. We both dug in at the Actor's Studio and studied as hard as anybody in town. During that time I was also studying at three other classes around town—discovering that each acting instructor had his niche, and sometimes these different points of view were worthwhile—but none, absolutely none, compared with the Actor's Studio. It was an honor and a privilege to be there.

Within a year after the audition at the Actor's Studio Alan had second billing in Al Pacino's first film *Panic in Needle Park*. He was named *Outstanding Newcomer of the Year in 1971* by Newsweek for his performance as a narcotics agent pursuing the drug-addicted Pacino. His reviews from coast to coast were wonderful.

While he was shooting that film I was shooting a film in Montana and Canada that starred Dustin Hoffman. I was on location for four months playing a West Point Lieutenant in a film about Custer's last stand called *Little Big Man*.

Hitting the Little Big Horn River at a full gallop while riding with Custer's 7th as hundreds of Indians from the Crow reservation (who had pulled the rubber tips from their arrows and had turned the sky black with them) were bearing down on us—well, those were days of heaven.

A few years later Alan and I starred in a film in which we played brothers, and again we drew on the huge warehouse of stored information that we had as brothers—the private jokes, the insane humor, the sibling rivalry, the private wars, most of which were unseen to the eye—even if you knew us well.

The *history of our relationship* was, as everybody said (and Quentin Tarantino still says) was a vital part of the film's success. The film, called *Macon County Line*, was a huge hit—not just in America, but internationally.

Alan and Jesse Vint in *Macon County Line*

The director, Richard Compton, was as insightful a director when it came to relationships as anybody I had ever seen. He saw in minutes what usually escaped the eye of others who had known us throughout our lifetime. He was highly aware and a gifted storyteller. He knew exactly how to tap into our innermost feelings and sibling rivalries. We were lucky—very lucky—that he was at the helm.

The bottom line is that (and I have seen this a hundred times) the most important facet of making a film or doing a play is that the actors connect organically. If that connection comes at the expense of interpretation of the material, it's okay initially. That organic response can then be shaped and sculpted by a good director who will provide his vision—but if there is no organic life, and only the director or actor's interpretation, then the film will probably lumber down the runway forever—never taking off —and end up a crashing bore.

I had another experience as an actor, where the *actual* relationship with another character in a film happened to be consistent with the demands of the screenplay. We both tapped into it, and the air definitely cracked with electricity when we worked with each other. The other actor's name was Timothy Dalton.

Just two days earlier, Timothy and I had gotten into a major fistfight on a hot July afternoon in Del Rio, Texas in front of the Holiday Inn, where the cast and crew of *Centennial* were staying. Universal was producing this twenty-five hour mini-series. Much of it was shot in Texas, but most of it was shot in Colorado.

To be as brief as possible, Timothy was shooting with the Colorado unit. My live-in girlfriend was also shooting there. She was a knock-out, and I never faulted any man for being attracted to her, or even making a pass at her. But once she would tell him to adios, and that she was in a committed relationship—if he didn't respect that and continued pursuing her, that's when I would step in. If she failed to make that clear to him—then I figured she wasn't my girlfriend after all, and I would have nothing to say about it.

Tim refused to back off, and eventually wrote her a crass letter that was meant to be insulting. She sent me the letter. When Tim came to Del Rio to work in the Texas unit, I introduced myself and asked him outside. Once outside I gently told him that it was unfortunate, but now I was going to have to beat the hell out of him, and that I had no choice in the matter.

Tim launched into a windy explanation about "mutual attraction" that made no sense. I finally interrupted and said, "If she was attracted to you, and you were attracted to her, then I probably would have never heard about this whole thing. Right, Tim?"

By this time many of the actors and stuntmen who were waiting to go out on location saw the exchange, and they began pouring out of the door of the Holiday Inn and gathering around. When this happened Tim became quite theatrical, like a Shakespearean actor playing to the back row, saying: "Let me put it to you this way. I will either take you inside and buy you a drink, Sir, or fight you to the death, whichever you prefer!"

I said, "How about we fight to the death." I slammed him in the chin with a straight right hand and he ran backwards twenty yards and fell on his back, with his legs straight up in the air. I thought he would be out for a week, but to my astonishment he jumped to his feet with enormous agility and yelled, "You sonofabitch! I'll kill you." He charged me like a bull, throwing punches and screaming. The actors and stuntmen then jumped in to block Tim and me, but they were getting punched, so they jumped out of the way and formed a ring, where Tim and I now began circling each other. There was another quick exchange, and I caught Tim with a left hook and he dropped to the ground. Once he scrambled to his feet, he was bewildered. He, as is the case with non-trained fighters, had no idea where that left-hook came from. He was warily circling me now, trying to figure out what went wrong. I leaped in with another left-hook and caught him flush on the chin. This time he collapsed as though he had been shot by a rifle and laid there completely motionless. People, including me, were getting nervous, but after a few more seconds he stirred, opened his eyes, and then held up his right hand, saying, "I've had enough."

I said, "Okay Tim, I can't afford to mark up your face and get fired, so this was round one, and round two will continue in six months, in November, when we both wrap."

Tim was big, athletic, fast, and he had heart—but he had either little or no skill. I did, and that's the *only reason* I was able to knock him cold.

As fate would have it, two days later Timothy Dalton and I were shooting a confrontational scene in the middle of the Texas badlands just a couple of miles from the historical Alamo. It started when he and two others rode out to my place and threatened me. Tim told me I had to get off the land. It was his now, he said. I told him, with rifle in hand, that I was a homesteader, and I wasn't leaving. The subterranean electricity between the two of us was as tangible a force as I've ever encountered as an actor. Both of us were tapped into that huge warehouse of information that is known as the sub-conscious. The scene was as effortless as any I've ever done. We avoided each other throughout the day, however. Neither of us wanted to ruin the venomous relationship we had with each other. It was perfect for the scene. The tension between us was noticed by everyone.

A couple of days later Tim did a very manly thing. The actors and stuntmen were having breakfast there at the Holiday Inn one early morning. It was just getting light outside. Sitting next to me was actor Les Lannom, and across from me were actors Glyn Turman and Greg Mullavy. All three were present during the fight. Tim walked up to where I was sitting, making everybody, including myself, very nervous, but he pleasantly and admirably surprised us all with these words:

"I was wrong, and if it were me, I would have done exactly the same as you. I hope you will accept my apology." He stuck out his hand.

I couldn't have been more surprised if a flying saucer had crashed into the swimming pool outside the Holiday Inn window. It was, for me, one of the most profound moments of my life. I learned something from Tim that day. He sat down next to me, we had breakfast, and we became friends after that. He was very bright, well read, charming, and a lot of fun. We played chess, and over drinks in Colorado, we talked about Jack London. Tim was/is a very interesting guy.

As "Amos Calendar" in Universal's *Centennial* from the book by James Michener.

USE OF AN EXISTING RELATIONSHIP

Timothy Dalton is another example of utilizing an *existing history* in the work with another actor. It can be very useful to utilize an existing relationship, but it can also backfire. Some actors have had love scenes with an actress that they are actually in love with. It can be very useful—but within a nanosecond, it can go awry. If the relationship happens to become cold and stormy just when you are called upon to be warm and loving, then you have to overcome a negative just to break even. That can be a real challenge, believe me. When I don't believe my own words, and I feel like I'm lying, I will curl up like a spider on a hot stove. I have to feel that I'm connected and telling the truth, or I will gasp for air and faint away. I'm not a natural performer. The only reason I was able to make a living as an actor is because I was so self-conscious and terrified of the audience that all of my resources were used to connect with my fellow actors. If my thoughts wandered out into the audience, even momentarily, I would immediately become self-conscious, my face would turn at first beet-red, and then a kind of dark maroon, and I would freeze.

In an odd way, this was a blessing. I knew I would be punished by those shades of red as few actors were if I did not tend to business. I had to focus on what I was trying to accomplish with my fellow actors in the scene. For this reason I strove, always, to make my fellow actors *the most important thing in the room while working with them*. There are ways to do this; I've already given two examples.

One of the reasons I initially studied acting was to get over my stage-fright. It never really went away, even after years of study and work as a professional. What happened was that through my training, I learned how to channel this energy along creative paths.

There is an old Russian proverb that I read in a Chekhov short story. I love it, and have never forgotten it. It said:

Chase two rabbits and you catch neither.

If an actor splits his concentration between the audience and his fellow actors, then usually he will neither connect with the audience, or his fellow actor—and he will most often flounder badly. I don't think you can ever go wrong by making your scene partner the most important person in the room.

As "Wolf" in Universal's *Silent Running*

Jack Nicholson said in an interview that one of the most difficult things for him in his early years as an actor was to *stop trying to please the audience*. This happens to be true of most actors. One of the ways to overcome trying to please the audience is to **act for yourself.**

I was doing an exercise with several others on stage at the Actor's Studio when Oscar winner Madelyn Sherwood leaned over to me and whispered, "*Act for yourself, Jess.*" She had caught me.

I gave this a lot of thought, believe me. A short time later I was at a museum looking at a Van Gogh original. I read that he had studied French Impressionism in France. It seemed to me that Van Gogh could have easily adopted this style at the time. French Impressionism was selling. It would have been easy for him. He could have sold a few paintings and put some money in his pocket; but he never did. Van Gogh *painted for himself.* To paint with a thousand percent of his soul—and never in his life sell a painting had to be a hell that was unimaginable. Yet he never whored himself out; he remained true to his vision to his dying day.

Every so often an actor comes along with the same kind of artistic dedication. Writer/director David Lynch is a favorite of mine for that very reason. These people, like Van Gogh, deserve their own galaxy.

STREAMLINING YOUR APPROACH

I mentioned earlier that after Dean and Brando's impact on the world film culture, thousands left their homes from all over the world and traveled to America to audition and study acting at the Actor's Studio. In Lee Strasberg's book *The Actor's Studio*, he mentions that only one in a thousand that auditioned there was allowed to study. I was one of the lucky ones. I studied there for many years in Los Angeles, beginning in 1968, following my study with Stella Adler in New York City. I spent many hours watching scenes performed by the very best actors in the business. The class would usually be from eight to midnight, with only two scenes performed. The scenes averaged around ten to fifteen minutes in length. The actors would then "talk about their work." They would tell the studio audience (which usually numbered anywhere from forty to sixty) about how they approached the material. Most of these actors were well known, and many of them had won or had been nominated for Oscars, Emmys, or Golden Globes. So out of two scenes totaling an average time of thirty minutes, the other three and a half hours consisted of the performers talking, and then the audience giving feedback. Finally, things were capped by the moderator—Lee Strasberg. If he happened to be on the east coast at the time, then any number of moderators would step in. Terrific actor Bruce Dern was always my favorite when Strasberg wasn't there. He was very insightful, but brutally honest.

Bruce would say things to the actors on stage such as, "You were bored to death up there ... and we were even more bored than you were!" He would say this while looking around the audience with a strange smile.

Oscar winner Shelley Winters amazed me. She was such a wonderful actress, but when explaining things as a moderator, totally incoherent. After listening to her for several years, I had the impression that she didn't have the slightest idea what she was talking about—she just did it. I guess it's possible.

Some people say that the left side of the brain is responsible for the organizing and structuring of your life. It is the calculating side, the chess playing side, the mathematical side, and the side that uses logic to make decisions. And they say that the right side of the brain is the creative side. When an artist decides that a touch of red is needed in this corner of his painting, there is no logical explanation for that choice. It is simply a creative choice and has nothing to do with logic. Shelley Winters, to me, had a right side of the brain that was the size of a cantaloupe, while the left side of her brain was the size of a raisin. In my mind, she was a totally creative person with no logic whatsoever—a kind of Jackson Pollack on stage.

There were a couple of others like this, but none as distinct as Shelley Winters. Her lack of logic never failed to entertain when she moderated. But perhaps this was an act. I have to say, however, that if it was an act, she continued this act everywhere she went—even over coffee.

But this I did know: Some actors dedicated their existence

to cluttering up their brains with every technical acting term, slogan, and exercise within a scene that you could possibly imagine. If they had been backpackers they wouldn't have made it one hundred yards without collapsing from the excess weight they were carrying. These actors were usually on the perimeter of professional acting, and it seemed to me that their purpose for doing a scene was ultimately and finally to be included in the world of acting at the Actor's Studio. So they would launch into a long technical explanation that served no real purpose except to sound hip—that they knew the work, loved it, and were dedicated toward the execution of it. They sometimes sounded like this one given by a lady one evening:

> *I first, in my preparation squeezed my familiar object, a tennis ball that I brought from home which was my golden retriever's before she died, then simultaneously inhaled the scent of bathroom freshener known as "lilac," which sensorially never fails to transport me to a time when I hid from my boyfriend in the bathroom. I, at the time, was trying to flee an entanglement. And then I did an emotional memory ... about something (tearing up) ... I can't talk about it, but it was there ... okay? So then I personalized my relationship with my stepson—who is, no other way to say it, pudgy, and particularized the scene itself, so that when I came to this line I then had the smell of a bad refrigerator to deal with that never really happened, and then ... well, (suddenly agitated) it just didn't happen ... okay? ... I mean I have the right to fail, don't I? I mean why are we here, if not to fail? Anyway, the sensory—it was a visual thing that never really happened, so I didn't panic. I just reached back in the purse and grabbed*

> the tennis ball. This familiar object is, most of the time, reliable, but this time ... what I'm saying is that in the end my intention became kind of like a Denver omelet with all kinds of stuff in it. It sort of misfired—it was a dud—so I guess I lost track about two-thirds of the way through the scene. So I found that my locator was running interference with a small knot of nervous energy that kept banging around inside of me like a pinball, and then surfacing in the neck area and causing it to jerk. Did anybody notice? ... I wasn't sure if it could be noticed, and that took me out of the scene momentarily, but my controller finally brought it under control, and then from there I felt that I hooked into something tangible and was off to the races, And after that everything seemed okay, but I know that I could do better ... I just don't know .... Anyway, that's it.

This sort of analysis would be followed by a long silence. People would make short perfunctory comments just to move the audience out of the sweltering heat that the explanation had generated. And then Strasberg would begin, and Strasberg could go on for a very long time without the slightest bit of consideration as to whether or not people found him interesting. This alone fascinated me about Strasberg more than any other single element of his character. People could nod out, fall out of their chair, and hit the floor right next to him, and it didn't seem to bother him one bit. One time I remember, it was after midnight, and he was still going on and on, and what he was saying was noteworthy for this reason; it had absolutely nothing to do with the actors on stage. They had been listening intently for over two hours, waiting for the cherished moment when his attention would turn to them and they could then bask in the glory of his genius, but the moment never came, and soon the actors on stage began to nod out along with the rest of the audience.

Sometimes I found myself reluctantly having a private thought: "This man is a genius all right; he is a genius at perpetuating a fraudulent image."

Vint as "Callahan" in *Bobby Jo and the Outlaw*

Part of that negativity that I felt toward him was because he was always dropping Brando's and Dean's names—constantly referring to them as "Marlon" and "Jimmy," when he had absolutely nothing to do with either one.

But there were other times when Strasberg could be absolutely brilliant, and I always admired him as a man who felt that he was the "keeper of the flame" of organic truth in acting, for he most definitely kept the Actor's Studio focused on the principles of Stanislavsky. This he did like nobody else, and if people tried to vary the curriculum in the slightest at the Actor's Studio, he became a tiger. I witnessed it several times.

The explanation that this lady gave about her work was certainly not typical at the Actor's Studio, but at the same time that type of explanation was not entirely unusual, either. The reason that some people loaded themselves up with so much technical thinking was that they felt that the mere knowledge of these things would bring them the magic they so desired to catapult them into the arena in which they craved to function. But as I worked more and more professionally, I learned from the very best actors in the business to *keep things both simple and clear*. When the really good actors—the ones who never failed to make an impact, both at the Actor's Studio and professionally—talked about their work there was a commonality to their approach: *everything had clarity*. There were only a couple of exceptions to this—one I've already mentioned.

LISTENING IS MANDATORY

I have seen people with handicaps and disabilities of all kinds in the entertainment business; but none is as handicapped as the person that doesn't listen to what others are saying. A person that can't listen to others will probably never overcome this defect. No matter how dedicated you are about breaking this information to them, they're probably not going to get it—because they're not listening. This type of person is usually waiting for you to pause so they can jump in with their life story—or most often they don't wait at all; they just talk over you. You've seen them. Everybody has—and everybody reacts in the same manner—to escape.

I know a guy in Los Angeles who is young, looks terrific, has a Porsche, a multi-million dollar house in the Hollywood Hills, and can't get a girlfriend, because he never hears a word that girls say to him. Whenever they try to tell him something, he talks over them. Now he cruises third-world countries, shopping for a mate. He finds them, too. The problem is that once they arrive in the U.S., it's only a matter of weeks until they bolt, flee, make their escape—diving into their ethnic sub-culture in L.A.—never to surface again. He can't understand it. I've tried many times to tell him—but he still doesn't listen; he just talks over me.

This guy made his money in real estate and sees acting as a way to meet beautiful women. He feels that once he becomes a famous actor his problems with women will disappear. But he doesn't have a chance as an actor — or with actresses. I once met a student born with a paralyzed face who has a far better chance than the person who can't listen. I don't think there is a single feature about a person that will lock them out of the world of film acting faster than the inability to listen.

When the cast is given a typed-up script, it's only a blue-print, really. It's an outline. The real information found in the subtext will be soaked up by the highly-aware actor during the rehearsals and the filming. The aware actor will listen in a way that he has never listened in ordinary life—because he knows that his livelihood depends on it. Once he develops a keen sense of listening, he will hear the words for the first time, even if the play has been running for months. He'll critically examine and re-examine the content of what people are saying to him, weighing and balancing, checking body language, observing the mercurial history he has with them. If he learns to do this then the amps that he receives from his partner will most certainly turbo-charge his performance, giving the scene the quality of a first occurrence. If he doesn't, there will always be a lack of harmony—a dead zone —a negative that the rest of the cast has to overcome.

There is not a single acting instructor in the world who doesn't recognize the value of listening. It's emphasized by everybody across the board as being mandatory.

Again, one certain way to listen intently is to find a way to make your scene partner the most interesting person in the room. In order to do this, you have to know what moves you, what gets you out of bed in the morning—you have to know your hot buttons.

THE PROBLEM OF ANTICIPATION

TRY this: Get together with a close friend or family member, think of a volatile subject, and then improvise an argument with a tape recorder running. Really go at it. If the neighbors call 911 you've probably done a great job.

Next, type up this improvised argument in screenplay form. If you don't know what screenplay form is, go to *scriptorama.com* or *simplyscripts.com* and find the screenplay of your choice.

Now, hand a copy of this screenplay to your friend. Both of you study your copy for as long as it takes to memorize it word for word. It could be two hours or two days, depending on the length of the scene and your ability to memorize.

Now, all the elements are in place, such as:

(a) Because it's you, then you are undoubtedly physically perfect for the part.
(b) The script that you improvised and typed up probably parallels some aspect of your life—something that you can relate to easily; otherwise you probably wouldn't have argued about it.
(c) So the question then becomes, who on this planet is

more perfect for this particular part than you? Probably nobody.

With this enormous advantage over all other actors across the globe you can now perform the typed-up and memorized scene with your friend and *tape that performance using a second and different tape.*

When you play back the two tapes there will probably be a world of difference between them. The first taped version, the one that was improvised, seems spontaneous and alive. The second taped version (the memorized and performed version) will most likely seem flat and lifeless, with a lack of spontaneity.

Why?

Because you probably were not surprised by anything your scene partner said once you had memorized your typed script. You knew what she was going to say; and she knew what you were going to say; and in some instances both of you were probably waiting for each other to say the next line so you could in turn say yours. Both actors were *anticipating* one another. Doing this guarantees a lack of spontaneity. When actors *anticipate* they don't truly *react* to one another, and they resort to *pretending to react.*

If an audience were only interested in the words of *Hamlet*, they could buy a copy of it for five dollars, stay home and read the play. They pay a lot of good money to see the play because they want to *watch the characters react in the situations*. That's why people drive a distance, look for a parking spot, stand in line in the rain, and pay a hefty price for a ticket. If the actors aren't reacting to the situations, or to each other, then the play simply won't work.

Jesse Vint as the evangelist "Victor Kruger" in the 2011
European film *Glory Jesus*

So by typing up an argument that you and your friend had, and then trying to perform it, you become critically aware of the actor's chief problem—*anticipation*. After all, even Shakespeare said, "*The anticipation prevents the discovery.*" And if he said it, it's probably true.

So how does the actor respond to something that he knows is going to happen? How does he *not anticipate*? First, let's say that you have been cast in a film. The script has you interrogating a person on page thirty. That character knows the whereabouts of a kidnapped family member, but on page thirty-two a gunman unexpectedly enters the room and puts a gun to your head.

How do you react with genuine surprise when the gunman enters? How do you *not* anticipate this?

Here's the answer: First, return to number one: *What is the character's problem?* If a family member has been kidnapped, and you have finally located somebody who knows where the family member is, then you must stay focused on extracting information from that person to find the family member. Your job as an actor is to not leave the room until you have this information that will free the kidnapped person—no matter what the script says. But this single feature is important:

> *You must have every expectation of success that your interrogation will yield the desired information. This guarantees that you will react when things go wrong.*

You must already be thinking about how you and your family member will be spending time together once he is freed—and what might happen if you fail to free him, and nothing else. If you are genuinely thinking these thoughts, and moving forward with every expectation of success, then you will be genuinely surprised when moments later a gunman suddenly steps out of a closet and puts a gun to your head.

Why?

Because only one thought can occupy your mind at a given time. You cannot walk a tightrope and do a complex math problem at the same time—or solve two math problems simultaneously—it's impossible.

If the actor stays focused on *solving the problem* of extracting information from the person he is interrogating on page thirty, *with every expectation of success, then that problem will occupy 100 percent of his mental real estate,* and he will react with genuine surprise when the gunman enters the room on page thirty-two. This is the only way I know of to solve an actor's chronic problem of anticipation.

PRECONCEIVING THE SCENE

PRE-conceiving a scene is the first cousin of anticipation. If you're thinking about the outcome, then more often than not your conscious mind will try to steer your being in that direction—and then you become the performing seal, who knows exactly what he is supposed to do—and is doing it by rote.

People who pre-conceive a scene rob themselves of the high of acting. How can you be taken by surprise with anything that is said and done when you are thinking about the scene as a choreographed result that is all laid out in front of you? You can't.

There is an old Viking saying found in the Icelandic Norse Eddas that was written over a thousand years ago that I love very much. In fact, I raised my son on it.

All you have to do in this life is try your best —the outcome is none of your business.

These beautiful words also apply to the art of acting. I always started my scenes by saying, *"I don't have the slightest idea what's going to happen here, but I do know that I have to find my kidnapped son,"* (or whatever your mission is). This helps to eliminate thinking about the outcome, or the pre-conceiving of a scene.

THE ULTIMATE HOT BUTTON

IT is also, of course, necessary to have the person who has been kidnapped mean everything to you. I found that if I imagined my son in any kind of danger, I was an unstoppable force, and there was not a power on the face of the earth that could discourage me. This, for me, was definitely a hot button that I hardwired to my mission over and over as an actor.

I made this discovery while working on *Macon County Line* after several years of professional work. Prior to that I was using, like most actors, my own life being in danger. But directors would sometimes say to me, "You have helicopters circling overhead; you're surrounded by twenty cop cars—your life is very much in danger, and you don't seem to care that much ...."

They were right. I wasn't exactly sure what to do about this. I have run out of air while scuba diving at a hundred and ten feet, had many narrow escapes on a motorcycle, been shot at several times, had an outraged husband put a .357 Magnum to my head, and oddly enough my heart beat simply slowed down while my brain accelerated like a Waring blender. Later, after these close calls, I had a philosophical cigarette, but I never really broke a sweat.

Things were very different when it came to my son. If he

were in the slightest bit of danger, then I would go berserk—and nothing could settle me down until I knew that he was safe again. I learned over time that I could always think of a way to hardwire my *mission* to the safety of my son—even if my part was to rob a bank. Now I would be robbing a bank so that they wouldn't pull the plug on a respirator that was keeping my son alive—so absolutely nothing could go wrong in this robbery. It put me in the zone every time. I felt as if I could go through a wall when it came to the safety of my son.

Friends of my son, Jesse IV, rented a restaurant in Los Angeles and threw him a huge birthday party. I flew to L.A. and called him from outside the restaurant. When he answered I told him how sorry I was that I couldn't make it down from Portland, Oregon. While talking to him, and wishing him a very happy birthday, I walked up behind him in the midst of his friends and tapped him on the shoulder. He turned around, cell phone still in hand, and an alert photographer caught the very emotional moment between father and son. His mother said that the joke was cruel, but she smiled anyway.

Once I discovered this, I would prepare by bringing out a

photograph of my son prior to the director saying, "Action," and tell my son not to worry about a thing. I found that this stirred the deepest feelings inside of me—and it had a 100 percent reliability rate.

In years of teaching, many of my students who had children learned how to do this when laying out their work as an actor—photograph and all—and it turbo-charged their performance every time. There are exceptions to everything, but I don't think that there is a stronger force in the entire animal kingdom than a parent's love for his or her children.

AN ACTOR'S RELAXATION

IT'S important. Stanislavsky devotes a great deal of time to relaxation. He believes that the actor's subconscious will never really be activated if he is overcome by nerves. He uses an ordinary cat as an example of an animal that is tightly focused, while their muscles are completely relaxed, even under stress. A cat seems to have the quality of boiling on the inside, while the outside is cool and relaxed. I could be way off here, but I have always believed that the expression "a cool cat," which evolved in the late 1940s and early 1950s, originated out of the ideal state of the Stanislavsky-trained actor—Brando being the ultimate bongo-drum-playing cool cat. Kerouac and Dean also fit prominently in there.

We used to spend an enormous amount of time at the Actor's Studio doing relaxation exercises. We were sprawled out in chairs on stage while the moderator would walk around and check for muscular tension by raising our arms or legs and then dropping them. Strasberg always said that the position to attain relaxation is the position that you find prior to dropping off and going to sleep, so that's what people did—they found that position and tried to go to sleep on stage.

It was incredibly boring—and it was supposed to be. That's how people were able to fall asleep. I found myself achieving that same sort of relaxation as a member of the audience, for I invariably found myself nodding out.

But here's what I learned through working professionally: it didn't matter how proficient I was at the relaxation exercises—if I wasn't completely prepared as an actor, I was terrified. I would be so nervous that my mouth would get dry and my lips would stick to my teeth. This actually happened to me once. It was the most horrible experience imaginable.

I learned over time that the only thing that truly relaxed me was the knowledge that I was the most prepared actor on the set. If I had this knowledge, I was relaxed. If I didn't feel as though I were totally prepared, I would be nervous. For me, it was that simple.

The key then, for me, was total preparation. I sometimes brought a friend on the set to rehearse with to find the elements in the scene that I could lock into 100 percent of the time—to isolate certain key moments and let them knock around inside of me—to try different personalizations, particularizations, and different hot buttons —and to study the person who would ultimately do the scene with me, accumulating data that would fire consistently.

I never really socialized much while on location. People were always asking where I was, and why I didn't hang out with everybody. The reason I didn't is because I was busy building a universe of people, characters, relationships, and places—and once I built them I tried to keep this universe pure, so that I could react to people and situations in a manner that was consistent with the character. I would frequently stay up all night rehearsing scenes with a plant, a doorknob, or a shower head while taking a shower. When walking down a street I would stop and rehearse with a tree. People thought I was nuts, but I soon accepted that it was just part of being an actor, and I also saw it as a way to test my concentration.

I have only had two reoccurring nightmares in my life. One is being re-drafted back into the army because they said they lost my records. In this dream I'm a geezer sitting in a foxhole with everybody staring at me and saying, "Why are you here?" I would explain that my records were lost, and that soon I would be released. Everybody would quietly puff on their cigarettes and stare at me—and then somebody would yell, "Incoming!" and a bomb would go off.

The other nightmare I still have, and it's far more terrifying, is that I'm riding out to location—completely unprepared. *I haven't even read the script*—nor can I find it—and I keep telling the first assistant director that I need a script, "so that I can go over a few things." He says okay— disappears—and I don't see him again. In the meantime the director has sent word that he wants to see the actors—to have a run-through. It is always the same dream in different forms.

I believe that preparation is always the key for relaxation. Sprawling in a chair to find a position that would cause me to readily doze off, I discovered, was not the key.

But one thing I believe that is universal is that nerves for the prepared actor are perfectly okay. You may rest assured that an athlete, after training for the Olympics for five years or longer, is nervous when his moment comes. Butterflies don't bother him, because he knows exactly which channels this nervous energy is going to flow through. His long and intense training has taken care of that. He knows that he needs it to win. Without this shot of adrenalin he will not be able to explode off the line, and he knows it. So he welcomes it.

It's also true of a well-prepared actor. He knows exactly where the nervous energy is going. His preparation has created corridors, so that when the dam breaks, everything floods into creative channels that he has created through training and preparation.

A thoroughbred horse is nervous. It prances sideways, kicks down a barn, spins in circles, but once it comes out of the gate you have poetry in motion. A plow horse is relaxed and seemingly without nerves, but there is no poetry.

I believe a talented actor is like the thoroughbred horse. Once the energy is directed properly you see something very nice.

Very often the finest performance for actors on Broadway is opening night for this reason. If they are ever going to fly like an eagle during the run, it will usually be on opening night.

SKILL, TALENT, AND THE GOOD AMATEUR

There is a difference between skill and talent. It's possible that a skilled actor can have no talent, and it's also just as possible that a talented actor can have no skill. In fact, this is true of any artist, musician, writer, etc.

A skilled actor is someone that has been acting for a while. He may have done summer theatre, or even Broadway, yet he may not feel a thing when he acts. He performs each individual line as it pops into his head with the confidence of someone that has been around. He is someone who has acquired the skill of essentially reading it out loud with a certain literary accuracy, even though the material has been memorized. He knows how to act the punctuation. The skilled actor with no talent has become skilled at pretending.

These people aren't always easy to deal with. Usually after a scene they turn to me with a huge smile on their face. They remind me of Oscar Wilde's saying:

People ask for criticism when all they want is praise.

They truly believe that they know what they're doing, and they're reluctant to listen to anybody. With these people I usually fire up the bulldozer and try to gently remove the bogus idea that they have about acting from their system. They usually don't like it and some never return. Their destiny is set: They are destined to remain the *skilled amateur*, and nothing more, because they have never learned how to internalize. I've seen this countless times in the last 40 years as an actor.

On the other hand, the talented actor with no skill or technique is like a rocket without fins. He's all over the place. He's almost always interesting to watch, because he is full of surprises, even to himself. The talented actor with no skill is very capable of living fully within the imaginary circumstances of the scene. They're novices, yet they come through the door with the very unique ability of self-inducing an organic experience. This kind of actor can be extremely bad or extremely good, sometimes within the same paragraph. The problem with this actor is that he has not developed a technique so that these volcanic feelings are channeled and controlled. Once he develops a technique so that his intense feelings are processed in a meaningful way, he will have true skill. The true skill, then, for the gifted actor, is the acquiring of a reliable technique to control the immense emotional life he or she has as a performer. Once he takes this step, his work on a professional level begins.

With this type of person my job is simply attaching fins to a rocket so that he or she has consistency and accuracy, but still maintains a degree of surprise and unpredictability.

Again, as an instructor I don't teach people how to act; I teach them how not to act.

A STRATEGY FOR THE EXTREMELY IMPORTANT, POTENTIALLY LIFE-ALTERING AUDITIONS

PREPARATION as an actor is usually the key *once you have been cast in the part*. You have a certain confidence in knowing that your audition worked and that everybody seems to think that you are right for the part. That knowledge helps your confidence.

Auditions, however, can have a much different temperament. Most actors are acquainted with the strange irony of being totally relaxed in auditions where you could care less whether or not you get the part, and then suffering a paralysis of mind, body, and soul at an audition when the dream part comes along. What does this mean? Does this mean that you are condemned to do uninteresting parts that you don't care much about—and then fall apart from stress during the auditions for the dream parts?

After blowing a super-important audition where I nearly fainted away and hit the floor, I came to the conclusion that there are times when the knowledge of a relaxation procedure is very useful. I was forced to admit that there were occasions in which being totally prepared would not always relax me. There is the huge audition that comes along once in a blue moon—the one that make it difficult for an actor to fall asleep the night before, the one that has the potential of being life-altering—and it is that audition that has given many actors a case of dry mouth. On this particular occasion my mouth turned bone dry, and I couldn't talk, because my lips were sticking to my teeth as if they had been covered in crazy glue. My only wish at that moment was to hit an ejection button and blast myself somewhere into outer space. It was horrible.

It only happened once, but I was determined that it would never happen again—and it didn't. I put together an audition strategy over the years that worked for me during times of super-stressful auditions. These are only suggestions. Again, you're an individual; what works for others may not work for you. You have to find the way that works best for you. Here are a few notes that I took after years of auditions.

(1) After blowing that audition, I learned a little about self-hypnotism, which is nothing more than a relaxation procedure that allows your body to function normally and your subconscious to function at a maximum. Self-hypnotism has to be learned and practiced, but in my experience it works. Hypnotism has nothing to do with being told to squeal like a pig or squawk like chicken. People don't do those things while hypnotized, unless that's what they want to do. Self-hypnotism brought me to a relaxed state as an actor when conditions were abnormally stressful. Many actors practice yoga for exactly the same reason. Worrying about whether or not you will be

relaxed for the audition is enough to guarantee that you will probably not be relaxed. During these times, if you have a procedure to turn to, it can be very helpful.

(2) Prepare the scene exactly the same way as you prepare a scene for a class or workshop. The difference is that you are doing a scene with the casting director instead of somebody from class. SAG rules say that actors must have the material twenty-four hours in advance, so there is time to do this.

(3) Many people hold the paper in front of them, even if they have the lines cold. For people that are new to auditioning, this would be recommended.

(4) *Take your time.* Go at 50 percent of production pace. If the scene partner asks you a question from the scene, repeat the question to yourself and think about the answer before answering. It's your audition; there is no hurry. Some actors are under the erroneous impression that to burn right through it demonstrates that they know the material really well and that they're super-prepared and ready to go to work.
Understand this: Anybody can memorize lines and burn right through it. People who have never acted before in their lives can do that. It means nothing. Take your time. Work with the casting director as though he or she is a scene partner in class.

(5) When reading with the casting director, make the casting

director (as the character) listen to you. As the character that you are playing, demand his attention without being unreasonable, obscene, or gimmicky. Sometimes casting directors get into a rut after auditioning all day, and they need to be jarred a little bit to get them out of it. Turn the tables on them if possible so they feel, to an extent, that they are an important part of the audition as well.

(6) Once you have completed the audition, politely say, "Thanks for having me in," and get the hell out. Don't try to hang around and socialize; they have work to do, and trying to hang around for feedback will deeply irritate them.

(7) Remember that you are not being judged on how you comb your hair, but on how effectively you borrow five dollars, interrogate a criminal, seduce a woman, persuade a jury, arrest a thug, or any number of missions that your character may have. That is what they will be looking for every time. That is what you prepare for and rehearse for; nothing else matters.

(8) Right before the casting director says, "Action," I always tell myself, "I don't have the slightest idea what is going to happen here, but I do know that before I leave this room, I will interrogate this criminal and successfully get the information that I need," (or whatever my mission happens to be). Over the years I have found that telling myself this allows the scene to go into undiscovered territory; it becomes new and fresh, and not the predictable

line of attack that the casting people have been seeing the greater part of the day. I also tell myself this after I have the part and am shooting the film.

(9) *Never* try to knock them dead. Knocking them dead is for fire eaters, trapeze artists, dog shows, and magicians. Remember, the character you are playing is not trying to be a good actor—he doesn't even know what good acting is. Just *talking* to the person that you're reading the scene with is never a bad place to start.

(10) When you go to an audition, there is a good chance that you will see fellow actors there. Stay away from them. Tell the secretary that you will be just outside the door in the parking lot, and ask if she would mind letting you know when your name comes up. Go outside and immerse yourself in the circumstances of the situation and stay there. If a fellow actor comes up and tries to start a conversation, just tell him that you have just received the material, you're not familiar with it, and you need this time to look at it. They will usually understand. No small talk with anybody! Save that for coffee shops.

These are several elements of my audition strategy that I have put together after working in the film business for several decades. I did not learn any of this out of a book, but only through my own experience as an actor. These strategies have worked for me, but others may have different strategies worth learning. You will find out, over time, which way works for you. Write it down so it becomes your *individual procedure* for auditioning, especially when it comes to the rare, life-altering dream part. It's those parts that can keep you awake at night in anticipation and then test your audition strategy when the time comes.

REHEARSALS

THIS was a favorite saying at the Actor's Studio when I was there.

Treat every performance like a rehearsal, and every rehearsal like a performance.

Our rehearsal time was usually spent *information gathering* to see what would work and what didn't work. Once the work was laid out, we would back off and let the scene come to us so the result would not be forced.

Again, Stanislavsky's lifetime of work concluded that an actor's subconscious should be activated in his work. The subconscious cannot be brow-beaten or forced into compliance. It can only be activated indirectly, and usually by gentle persuasion. *Forcing the result* almost always leads to a kind of play-acting, like a couple of small children playing cars in a sandbox.

Actor's ways and methods of rehearsing vary enormously, so all I will do here is talk briefly about what I have seen from some of the very best actors in the business in terms of rehearsal.

Very often the culprit standing between an actor and his personal best performance level is concern over the lines. The character he is playing doesn't worry about the lines, and the actor shouldn't either. To solve this problem, he should learn the lines cold. If an actor knows his lines backward and forward, if he knows them to the point where he could juggle oranges while saying them without a single pause, then his mind is free to roam the sub-text, fastening on to the elements that his character is concerned about. This is the way it should be. If an actor's mentality is simply scanning for lines, then he is no longer involved in the situation. His belief dries up, and he finds himself wishing he were somewhere else.

Running the lines rapidly with no performance at all will usually expose the areas where you are having trouble with the lines. It's good to find this out. The one thing you will notice is that if there is a problem, the problem usually occurs at exactly the same place every time. Circle that spot, isolate it, and work on it separately. Very often there is a dramatic transition that is occurring there that the actor has failed to notice—and so to him it doesn't flow—it seems like a non sequitor. Study it carefully. You will probably find that once you understand the reason for the transition, then the problem will disappear.

The purpose of all rehearsals is to forget that there was ever a rehearsal.

The purpose of rehearsing is to immerse yourself deeper and deeper into the situation with each rehearsal until finally you no longer feel that you are acting—that you effortlessly find yourself trapped in a predicament that you are trying to get out of. Reaching that level is the actor's nirvana. It's a great feeling, especially when it happens in front of the camera.

Nobody worked harder than Marlon Brando when he decided to roll up his sleeves. He was a genius whenever he wanted to be. But when he was not inspired, he was essentially lazy, as he candidly described himself in his book *Brando on Brando*.

Brando, in his later work, was sometimes known for pasting his lines around the set, so that he wouldn't have to memorize them. By doing this his mind was then free to roam the sub-text. It was free to be gripped by the situation, the predicament, the crisis. The point of mentioning this is to corroborate the idea that when the actor is consumed by struggling to remember the lines he simply cannot function—even if the actor is Marlon Brando.

Try this. Buy a small voice-activated tape recorder. Take a two character scene and have someone else record the other person's lines as you run through the scene. Your lines should be mouthed silently. Now, when you play it back, you can hear the other person speaking her lines to you, and then you can respond with your lines. This is a good way to run the lines in your car on the way to work. Running lines with a tape recorder will also help you sharpen your response time on your cues.

Of course, no matter how well you think you are prepared, looking someone in the eyes for the first time during a rehearsal can change everything—as it should.

Here's a really good exercise. Learn Hamlet's advice to his acting troupe that begins with: *Speak the speech, I pray you, as I pronounce it to you, trippingly on the tongue* ....

Some say that it was Shakespeare who invented the human being. While that may be up for debate, almost nobody doubts that he was the greatest literary mind that has ever lived. This alone is a good reason to memorize his thoughts about acting, so that they are close to your heart at all times—for life.

It is several pages long. You can find it on the Internet by Googling the first sentence. Learn it word perfect. And no matter how well you know it, never lose sight of who you are talking to and why. Never forget that Hamlet demands of his actors that this play has to be pulled off perfectly with the actors "holding as it t'were, the mirror up to nature." No strutting and bellowing, and sawing the air thus on this performance!

This, of course, was Shakespeare advising his actors on how he wanted his plays performed, now and forever. He was simply tired of hack actors butchering his works. He hoped that this monologue by the prince would put a stop to it.

Once you can do this monologue word-perfect straight through without any pauses whatsoever, then you are ready to relax, explore the sub-text, feel the grip of the situation, and think of things that go far beyond performing as an actor. You are ready to seek out a creativity that travels into the deepest recesses of your soul. This has nothing to do with pleasing an audience. It has to do with *acting for yourself.* I do this monologue all the time, but only for me—just for myself. It never fails to bring something to the day.

The point of telling you this is to remind you that when your mind is free to roam and explore the subtext, and not be shackled by worrying about the lines, then acting can be truly a great adventure. In my opinion, there's nothing like it.

It's also important to note that some actors have said, "Don't learn the lines too well … that way you will always be struggling for the right words … just like a real live human being."

This is probably true. Many people have told me that James

Dean supposedly said this. However, James Dean could afford to go off script—because it was his name that put the deal together.

I have worked in situations where the writer was on set conferring with the producers—on every word. *Earthquake* was one of those films. Every time I said my dialogue, and I was slightly off, the producer or director would tap me on the shoulder and say that I said "those guys ..." instead of "those fellows ...."

If your name has inked the deal, then that probably won't happen. If not, then I have found that there is an advantage to learning it word perfect.

Sometimes improvisation is desired by the producer and director. While filming *Macon County Line* my brother Alan and I improvised continuously, throughout the entire picture. It was always a lot of fun, until the script girl approached me and said, "Okay, we have to match this with your close-up and so here's the dialogue ... and you said this while doing that, and you did that while saying this ... and so on." Now we had to struggle to match the previous takes, not just with dialogue, but with the same freshness and spontaneity that we had earlier—and that was not always an easy thing to do.

Sometimes the director will play the entire scene on a two-shot. That way you don't have to match anything. You'll see a lot of scenes played on two shots in Woody Allen films. His dialogue is the best, in my opinion, and perhaps he doesn't want it wrecked by actors struggling to match their previous takes.

PREPARATION BEFORE THE DIRECTOR SAYS, "ACTION"

WHEN actors do a play in the theatre, they usually are not deeply immersed with the complexities of the circumstances within the first few seconds, because the complexities have not yet unfolded. In the first act they are simply introducing the characters and setting the stage for the conflict. Stage actors always begin the day's work on the same page—and that's page one.

Film acting is very different. Ninety percent of the time, the film actor is not starting the day's shooting on page one, as in theatre. For example, he may be starting the day's work on page seventy, where he learns that his kidnapped wife has been killed. He may be expected to have a meltdown on, "Action." If so, then he does not have the luxury of a grace period for the scene to pull him in. This is one of the main distinctions between film acting and theatre. A film actor must be ready to deeply immerse himself in the circumstances of the screenplay *before* the director says, "Action," *on any page in the screenplay.* In short, the film actor's soul must be on fire *before* the director says action.

As "Insane Wayne" in the "Insane Wayne" episode of ***The A-Team***

Artist's rendition of Vint as "Tulsa Jack"

If an actor has a particularly challenging scene for the day's shoot, the first thing he has to do is to tell the first assistant director to keep him informed as to how much time there is before this scene is shot. The actor must prepare himself for this challenge long before the crew is ready to shoot it. He must be ready to descend into dark and painful areas (or whatever the challenge is), and churn these areas on cue. Many actors, on such challenging days, will isolate themselves from the rest of the cast and crew so they can stay in the zone and not be pulled out of it with small talk.

Some actors will prepare by listening to specific music that never fails to inspire certain feelings, thoughts, and emotions. Actor Lonny Chapman, who worked with James Dean on *East of Eden*, once told me that James Dean used to prepare for a particularly emotional scene by listening to Richard Wagner's classic *Ride of the Valkyries* over and over, while slowly sipping red wine. I had also heard this from someone else who worked with Dean—Corey Allen.

Many actors at the Actor's Studio would take recorded music of their choice to the set with them. Music, for sure, has the extraordinary ability to immediately catapult a person into a certain zone with pinpoint accuracy as well as anything.

Whatever you do, just remember that in all scenes, but particularly the challenging ones, *90 percent of your work as an actor is done before you say a word.*

COMMON TRAPS FOR ACTORS

THE single most common trap for actors is the desire to be terrific while acting. Even top pros step into this trap—sometimes over and over again.

Trying to be a good actor: Actors are by nature competitive. They like to win. They like to be good at what they do. In the world's most competitive profession, they naturally struggle to excel. There is nothing wrong with that—except for one thing—*the characters they are playing are not trying to be good actors.*

The characters that they are playing are trying to find a criminal, run from the law, seduce a beautiful girl, overcome a physical handicap, climb Mt. Everest, dynamite a relative off of the sofa, mend a broken heart—any number of things—but they are never trying to knock people dead through their acting.

The character he is playing may be trying to do many things, but being a good actor is definitely not one of them.

So avoid acting contests with other actors. Don't show off your acting skills. Once that begins you have fallen into the trap.

Acting the storyline: Another common trap for actors is to act the story line. The pressure of professional work can drive an actor to do this. I'll say it again: *It is never the actor's responsibility to tell the story.* The director is the storyteller. The actor is on a mission to accomplish something. This mission has nothing to do with acting the storyline.

Playing a quality: Usually the actor knows why he was hired. He might be there to terrify bank customers, to persuade a union to go on strike, to charm the leading lady— any number of things. On a major film there is an enormous amount of money at stake with each tick of the clock. Sometimes the production company can only secure a particular location until noon; after that they have to move out, no matter what. The location might be a bridge that crosses a river, or a train station, or any number of things that require adhering to a tight schedule.

As "Father Henry" in the 2011 film
Sister Mary's Angel

So the actor very much wants to please the director and producer who hire him by delivering the goods that he knows he was hired to deliver *on the first take,* if possible. In this case it's tempting for the actor to *play a quality* that he knows that he has to move the story forward. If he's a bad guy, he snarls; if he's a good guy, he proceeds with a captivating smile that he knows he has, or whatever it is. The actor feels the pressure of the huge production deadline, and so he tries to be a soldier and do things right for the production company. He hears the director say "That's a print! Let's move the camera over here, please." He's relieved—until he sees the movie and discovers that he whored himself out on that take by "playing a quality," and now it's immortalized. Too bad. What should he have done?

The remedy under this kind of pressure is to have your mission clearly defined. Stanislavsky emphasized over and over that when your focus wanders outside the circle of attention, (in this case the producer and director who are standing behind the camera and fretting over time problems) then you are most definitely in the erroneous zone. The character that you are playing knows nothing about trying to please the director, the producer, or anybody else. He is on a mission to get information out of this criminal and he will not leave the room until this happens—period. The criminal you are interrogating is the most important person in the room to the character the actor is playing—not the producer and director.

It is easy to buckle under this kind of pressure. I've seen good actors mechanically run through a scene because the sun was setting and crew members were yelling, "We're losing light." The panic that the production hierarchy feels is sometimes then passed onto the actor.

The actor can please both himself and the production hierarchy by defining his mission precisely, *internalizing* that mission, and consequently making the achievement of that goal the most important thing in his life. Ultimately he cannot waiver from organic truth—no matter what.

THE POTENTIAL TRAP WITHIN CHARACTER WORK

WHEN an actor is cast in a part that is physically, culturally, morally, and ethically different from him, then he still has to activate his soul when he does the part. Many people have the erroneous view that to do character work requires that they completely conceal their true identity from the audience, and manufacture emotions that they feel are consistent with the character. If this were the case, then professional impressionists would be working continuously in "A" films. Many professional impressionists can do any walk, any talk, and contort their faces and beings in the most amazing ways. The problem with that is, while entertaining, it's not believable if they are asked to play a real character. The impressionist doesn't know how to internalize, and without internalizing the actor has nothing. This approach guarantees a hollow performance that moves no one.

It's a matter of aesthetics, and aesthetics is often a matter of individual taste, but to me, Marlon Brando exemplified the ultimate character actor with astonishingly diverse characterizations, such as "Terry Malloy" in *On The Waterfront*, or a Nazi soldier in *The Young Lions*, or "Johnny" in *The Wild One*, or "Marc Anthony"

THE POTENTIAL TRAP WITHIN CHARACTER WORK

in *Julius Caesar*, or as "Don Corleone" in *The Godfather*, and many others.

Brando showed us to the core who these characters were, but it was still, at the core, Brando's heart and soul. It was as though Brando approached the character by saying, "If I had been born and raised as this character in this time and place, how would I walk and talk? How would I think? What would I hold dear? What would I despise? What would I fight for? He did not try to hide his identity from the audience. There are actors who believe that they are successful as a character actor if they completely hide their identity from the audience. If they approach the character without internalizing, whose heart and soul are we then seeing? The truth is, we aren't seeing anybody's. That sort of characterization is soulless. There's a name for it—it's called *externalizing*.

This is a common trap for actors. Character work, no matter how extreme, has to be internalized also. The physical modifications should not come at the expense of a strong internal life. If this happens, then the audience is seeing an impressionist at work—not the character.

I admire character work as much as anybody, but I have seen many an actor who believes that strapping on a fake nose, walking with a limp, changing the voice, and screwing up the face is character work. But without internalizing, that's not character work—that's Halloween.

One of the greatest examples of character work that I have seen in recent years is Heath Ledger's performance as "The Joker" in *Batman*. I am very rarely astonished by a performance—but that performance astonished me. I felt that, not only was I seeing a unique internalized character, but I felt that I was seeing the entire history of the character every time he said a line. The last time I had that feeling was while watching Charlize Theron in *Monster*. Other such outstanding characterizations include Michael Parks in *Kill Bill 2*, Marlon Brando as "Don Corleone" in *The Godfather*, Marlon Brando in several other films, Richard Widmark as "Tommy Udo" in *Kiss of Death*, and Robert Newton as "Long John Silver" in *Treasure Island*, to name a few.

When people begin acting, I always encourage them to find parts that are close to their own physicality and value system. Once they begin to find themselves in the grip of story predicaments, then they can begin to alter their physicality's to meet the demands of character identity without the actors losing their own strong emotional lives. After all, the actors are ultimately pushing their own hot buttons, not the hot buttons of fictional characters that don't exist.

If beginning actors want to do an accent, then I always advise them to "suggest" an accent, otherwise a full-blown accent will very often lead to doing an impression of an Irishmen, or a New Yorker, a southern Baptist preacher, or a French Canadian. A full-blown accent done by a beginner almost always leads to generalizing, which pretty much guarantees that we will see all of the well-known clichés of the character.

Once an actor has found the strong internal life of the character, and ideas of the physicality begin to challenge her, then I have found nearly 100 percent of the time that if an actor then takes her character to the streets and begins to function with that physicality, accent, and way of relating to others, she will greatly enhance her believability when the time comes to hit her mark.

I advise that actors shop *in character* for their clothes at Goodwill, ask directions around town, talk to people who are walking their dogs about their dogs (which is usually welcomed),

THE POTENTIAL TRAP WITHIN CHARACTER WORK

and on and on. If the actor stays in character around town for several days, or even several weeks, then these elements of character soon become *second nature*, as they should be. The actor shouldn't have to be thinking about her accent or her unique physicality any more (or any less) than the character is thinking about these things. She should only be thinking about how to escape the predicament she's in.

Also, in the streets she will soon get a sense of what is working and what is not, because the accent and the physicality of the character are now being flight-tested.

When an actor gets to the set, she should hang out only with people and in places where she can comfortably stay in character. I never demand this, but I like it when people on the set refer to me only by my character's name.

Many years ago, I used to know a stunning girl by the name of Debbie Feuer. She later married an up-and-coming actor by the name of Mickey Rourke. They came to see me in a play about six months later, and afterwards we went out. Debbie's sister, Tammy, was also there. Later, with Mickey sitting right there, Debbie told me that she never knew who she was married to until she read Mickey's next script—and then that's who she would be married to for the next six months. Mickey thought that was funny—but Debbie didn't seem too happy about it. They divorced a year later.

But it was interesting to me, because I had heard exactly the same thing from Nick Nolte's wife a couple of years earlier out on Triunfo Road.

One day I drove up in Nick's front yard, and he was going through some weird motions. I asked him what he was doing, and he answered Thai Chi (I think). I reminded him that I had read the script and I didn't remember a place where he did Thai

Chi. He said there wasn't one, but that his character knew Thai Chi, and so he had to not only learn it, but discover why it was a necessary part of his character's life. He resumed his work, even though the work that he was doing would never appear in the film. I admired Nick's intense dedication as an actor. I walked over to his wife— a surly blonde who was leaning against the door jam and waving a cigarette while talking. "Hell I never know who I'm married to until I read Nick's next script." she said, with a nicotine rasp in her laugh.

Of course there is certain insanity about all of this, but maybe that's why it's so much fun.

WORK WITH THE PLACE

WORKING with the place where you are located is an important element of acting that is usually overlooked. The truth is that a scene with the exact same characters, situation, and dialogue goes much differently on a space station than in an Eskimo village, or Death Valley, or a prison, or a high school. These locations are all stimulating in different ways. Directly or indirectly, in every case, location will affect the outcome of the scene. The awareness of *place* is always highly important.

Location is a particularly prominent factor when a character is at odds with his environment—such as a homeless man who has been invited to have dinner in a mansion, or a European Queen traveling through parts of Africa. In some cases it becomes the mainspring of the story—such as *The Wizard of Oz*.

The place ideally becomes another character in the story that is continually under investigation by the actor. The actor, regardless of what is happening, almost never stops investigating the premises.

Why?

It could have to do with the safety of his character, or a natural curiosity he has about his surroundings, but usually it has to do with why he is there in the first place—and what the actor's mission is.

For example, if an actor is playing a character who thinks that his best friend is having an affair with his wife, then when he enters his friend's premises, and while (seemingly) talking about unrelated subjects, his mind is scanning the place for any sign of evidence that his wife has been there—and this never stops. It is done in tandem with a psychological scanning of his wife's love interest.

The script may say nothing about this, by the way, but it doesn't matter. This is part of the actor's work.

If an actress is playing a girl on a date and her boyfriend brings her over to the condo for the first time, then she will probably be scanning his bookshelves to see what kind of books he reads. If most of them are cookbooks, then that's one kind of guy; but if they are DVDs of UFC title fights, then that's another clue as to who this prospect is. Are there books by Nietzsche, or Gandhi? That will tell you something about who you're dealing with.

What pictures are on the wall? Are there any of family? Other girls? Any art? Are they all pictures of himself in former days of glory? Who is this guy?

This is not just the art director's work; this is the actor's work as well.

Receiving creative energy from your partner is highly important. Working with the place is a continuation of receiving information about your partner and your mission.

James Dean under the tutelage of Elia Kazan did this as well as anybody I've ever seen, and that was a half-a-century ago. He never stopped investigating the premises to learn about who he was dealing with. Not only was it very interesting to watch, but it also busied the actor with discovering elements that had to do with why he was there in the first place.

If you take an ordinary cat and drop it on the floor of a strange house, watch it investigate the premises. No actor can top an ordinary housecat when it comes to investigation of the premises—but James Dean came close.

At Stella Adler's, Gene Frankel's, and the Actor's Studio we did a lot of exercises on this alone—investigating the place, and allowing it to affect us while doing the scene. For me, they all paid off.

Many exercises proved (for me) to be a waste of time— but *working with the place* was never a waste of time.

Working with the place also takes you out of the audition room during auditions where judges are sometimes sitting there with a scowl on their face and their arms folded.

The following suggestions are based on the way some of us proceeded. It begins with why you are there in the first place. You have to know this with absolute clarity, and then you can begin your information gathering.

Let's return to Stanislavsky's cat: He's usually in the strange place against his will, and when he is dropped on the floor, he begins the search for elements that could mean danger. The cat, ultimately, is worried about its own safety.

Ultimately, the actor playing a character is worried about the same thing. If he is gathering information, it is absolutely for his peace of mind—his safety—his knowledge of whether this person is adversarial or on his side. He can learn a lot.

If it's a workshop scene in an acting class, and there is nothing on stage except a table, a sofa, and a couple of pillows, it is perfect. Your imagination will supply the rest.

Start by functioning in your own kitchen at home, downloading as many visuals, sounds, and smells as you can. Then walk into an adjoining room and see just how much of this you can re-create for yourself. Keep doing this over and over. Soon you'll cut a glide path for this kind of work. It will become a continuous source of energy and information for your being as an actor while performing—for the rest of your life. It will become second nature to you by the time you return to your acting workshop. The premises will no longer be a bare stage with a few items scattered around to remind you that you're being judged in a workshop; it will be a functioning place that helps kick-start your creativity.

Many actors have asked me the same valid question: "But if you are at the location—say the Utah Salt Flats, then it's already there, so why do you have to imagine it?"

The answer is that you don't—but there is a huge difference between the actor who is, like a cat, completely aware and investigating and responding to his environment, and another actor who is standing there like a lethargic plow-horse with his head drooped in the burning mid-day sun. The two can't be compared.

It's not easy to get some students to delve into *working with the place* for this reason—they don't see the relevance. They seem to be asking themselves, "What does all this have to do with being admired?"

All I can say is that this is part of the road of *learning to act for yourself*. Once you have done that, then by that one feature alone you have separated yourself from the massive glut of humanity that oozes out of the Greyhound Bus terminal in Hollywood every day to become rich and famous.

RELATIONSHIP WITH THE CAMERA

IF you've ever had somebody around you who was slavishly devoted to you, who you didn't give a damn about, then you know how to regard the camera. The idea is to be aware of its presence, to respect the efforts of its operators, but never to feel the inclination to tailor or adjust your performance in a manner that you feel will enhance your standing with the millions of viewers who are looking through the camera's eye. That road will take you over a cliff. It is not organically pure to act for the camera. If the director says to make certain adjustments for the moves and focus of the camera, it's your job to find a way to justify these moves internally, so that you are not acting for the camera, and that you are still *acting for yourself*. The character is not acting for the camera, and you shouldn't be either.

For example, let's say a director tells you that when you walk through the kitchen doorway—that's when you discover your best friend making out with your wife—and at that moment he wants to zoom in *beyond an extreme close up*, framing only your eyes. So, he needs you to hit your exact mark, to the millimeter. If this is what the cinematic storyteller (director) wants, then you have your work cut out for you.

Two things must occur: First, the precision on the stop (hitting your mark) is mandatory for correct camera focus. Secondly, the internalizing of one of the worst things that can happen to you at that precise moment is also mandatory. Your job is to sync the two.

While they are lighting the scene for the camera, the first thing you do is to practice the move over and over as you walk through the doorway so that your mind becomes freed from the enormous burden of having to think about a camera move. On moves like that I sometimes act as my own stand-in. This gives me additional time on set for measuring with my eye and setting certain marks so that *the move becomes second nature*. The mind becomes freed from the harness of the move, and now you can get down to the business of retaining organic purity.

Secondly, this is a moment that shatters your character's belief in the universe as he knows it. All trust is gone. There is nothing left. It's a severely painful moment, and requires that you find a compartment inside yourself that you possibly have sealed off tightly for a very good reason—the pain was excruciating. Now you have to descend into that cellar to open that door and access it once again. It requires a separate exercise, and lots of hard work, so that it can be accessed on cue. The exercising of this moment over and over is, in effect, building an *internalized glide path* so that the powerful moment can occur on cue.

As country singing star "George Randall"
in NBC's *XXX's and OOO's*

At the Actor's Studio these separate exercises were known as *emotional memories*. Stanislavsky's book *An Actor Prepares* will take you through these separate exercises as well as any book that has ever been written.

When you find a key moment in a script, such as a decision made by the character that alters the course of his life, and maybe the world, such as Bogart's decision to help the French underground escape Casablanca, after proclaiming throughout the film that he "never sticks his neck out for anyone," then this sizable moment most likely requires a separate exercise. This supremely powerful moment will probably not occur on the depth that is necessary by just randomly running the lines. To have this moment occur simultaneously with a *precision camera move* demands that the moment be practiced and rehearsed in advance. A Meisnerite, however, will tell you differently.

And while we're at it, let me address an issue: **The unfortunate glut of Meisnerite frauds.**

Meisner has blessed us with a great exercise, and that's about it. It is not a technique.

When you hand a Meisnerite a script, they don't know what to do or how to proceed. If they do, they didn't learn it studying Meisner.

Here's the plus side to Meisner: Meisner knew that a good part of the actor's problem is his natural tendency to focus on the lines. In many cases, when you see the actor struggling, his struggle is to remember which line is which, and what to say now, and how to say it. The character that he is playing is not familiar with any of these struggles. Meisner developed a good exercise designed exclusively to find the life below the lines, to develop a keen awareness of the person with whom he is interacting, and to free himself from the shackles of thinking about lines at all. The experience of what acting is then becomes seared into the actor's being, so that he now strives for that sensation of not relying at all on the lines to do the work for him.

For example, the repetition exercise gives absolutely no value to the lines themselves, such as:

"I have a green shirt."
"You have a green shirt."
"I have a green shirt."
"You have a green shirt."

After a short time the actors begin focusing exclusively on each other, and responding to each other, rather than trying to interpret the material and inject a meaning into the lines themselves. The lines, like a word that's repeated over and over, soon lose meaning entirely. There clearly is no interpretation of the material in this exercise, and there just as clearly is no value or meaning to the lines. There is no struggle to remember lines, and no effort to be sensational, or inject meaning that is not there, because the lines mean absolutely nothing. The consequence is that the actors only have one another to relate to, focus on, and ultimately to react to. When an actor reaches this point, it's a milestone. *It's very valuable—as a single exercise.*

Here's the minus side to Meisner: Like the hamster in the wheel, Meisnerites will end up doing these repetition exercises until they're punchy. They eventually come to pride themselves on their ability to vary the "I have a green shirt" line two hundred and forty-six different ways while working with their partners—sometimes being a hot-head, other times being adorable, but always being hopelessly delusional that they have finally discovered themselves in their art. It's truly only a means to an end—but most Meisnerites see it as the absolute end. They're wrong. Here's why: The Meisnerite, after several months (sometimes years) of doing this type of exercise, now ventures into the world of auditioning. This is usually where he hits the wall, for this reason:

Auditions usually isolate the most challenging scene of the film to test an actor's ability. If the audition were for the film *Casablanca*, the audition scene would probably be the scene where Rick has to make the torturous decision to help his underground friends escape—and reverse everything that he has grown to stand for over the years.

During the auditions the producer and director are usually thinking that if an actor can pull off this very challenging scene, then the rest of the scenes for that actor would be relatively easy. If they can't find an actor who can pull this scene off, then they don't have a movie—pure and simple.

In almost all films a lead character, at some point, has to have a melt-down, make a momentous decision, confront evil, and so on.

The Meisnerite is at a disadvantage because he has never learned how to isolate and internalize key sections in the script, or in any way be responsible toward the most challenging areas of the script.

Many out there will disagree with me—but for those of you who do disagree, please consider why Sanford Meisner (on his DVD) can cite only two actors who have gained prominence from his teachings—after teaching acting for over a half-a-century?

Furthermore, these two actors, Pollack and Rydell, aren't even known for their acting; they are known as directors. Neither of these two directors was ever outstanding as actors. They were simply better than directors usually are when they have cast themselves in their own films.

It is true that several actors, like Steve McQueen, studied Meisner briefly; but they always seem to, like McQueen, move on to places like the Actor's Studio, where the principles of Stanislavsky are held in reverence. The Meisnerites, however, will boast for decades that, "We taught Steve Mcqueen." It's simply not true.

So why is the film business suddenly clogged with a glut of Meisnerites? Here's why:

Meisner wrote a book, detailing his approach, his exercises, and also the comments and critical examination of students performing those individual exercises. This has paved the way for fraud in the acting business, because now we have people across the world that *have never made a dime as professional actors*—and they are now teaching acting simply because they've read Meisner's book. They're everywhere! In Los Angeles they are almost as plentiful as automobiles. These instructors take the exercises directly out of Meisner's book, and also make their instructional comments right out of the book, whether the comments apply to that particular student's work or not. I have audited over forty acting classes in the last forty years, and this is a reality that is very consistent. I was forced to come to this conclusion:

> *Simply put, some of these people are imposters, and learning acting from them is tantamount to learning acting from the sailor who has never been to sea, the soldier who has never been to war, or the cowboy who has never ridden a horse.*

Again, I fully agree that Meisner has developed a very good

exercise to learn how to connect with your partner, which is a vital part of the acting process, but the actor should move on to the principles of Stanislavsky if he wants to learn in-depth acting.

In conclusion, I strongly believe that newcomers should always check out the IMDB before studying with anyone to see exactly what their credentials for teaching are.

THE INTERNET MOVIE DATA BASE

One incredibly positive development is the Internet Movie Data Base (www.imdb.com). This is a great tool for ferreting out frauds. The IMDB is an independent monitoring unit that somehow knows more about my career than I do. If an actor has done anything at all, it will usually be revealed on the IMDB. The problem is that newcomers who are straight off the Greyhound bus are unaware of it, and don't know how to check out the fraudulent teachers.

There is however, as of late, another problem that has surfaced regarding the IMDB. Some technogeeks have developed the unusual skill of putting their backyard video tapes of their moms throwing Frisbees to their pet whippets on the IMDB as a film that has played internationally, and even rating them as winning films. They have somehow found a way to circumvent the fine mesh net of the IMDB to fabricate credentials. This problem will continue to expand as video cameras and computer editing equipment give any fourteen year old the ability to make a film in his garage.

CASTING DIRECTORS

CASTING directors have been supplementing their incomes by opening acting classes for some time now. They fall into a totally different category than the fraud that has never done anything. A casting director's comments can sometimes be very valuable for the actor.

A casting director's job is to supply the producer and director with a talent pool of suggestions for each character. He has accumulated this list by watching everything he possibly can—by going to plays and by keeping his ear to the ground. Sometimes he is in direct contact with acting instructors whose eye he trusts. Those acting instructors will call him and say, "You have to take a look at this actor. She's on fire." In such a case that actor will probably get a call. The casting director will have the actor bring in a short two-minute scene that can be performed with the partner of the actor's choice in the office. The casting director will take a few pictures, make notes, probably video them, chat briefly, and then send them on their way.

The casting director doesn't make the final decision about the casting of a role. The producer and director make that decision. He cannot get you the part, but he can keep you out of the casting session by simply saying that he has heard that so and so has some bad habits—likes to argue, and is sometimes unprepared, for example. Once a casting director gets that in his mind, that negativity is usually there for life.

Casting directors usually can't teach acting, although that doesn't prevent them from offering acting classes. They can tell you what they like; and they can tell you what they don't like. Generally, though, they can't tell you how to do it, because they don't know. If they knew, in my opinion, they'd be actors. There are exceptions to this, but they are rare.

However, I have to say that once you have studied with a legitimate acting instructor, then enrolling in a casting director's class can be highly beneficial for two reasons. First and foremost, you expose yourself and your talent to a casting director. I have always said:

> *It is not who you know; it's who knows you, and your ability as an actor.*

It's *your responsibility*, and nobody else's, to make sure that there are people out there who know what you can do as an actor. Enrolling in a casting director's class is certainly a legitimate way of exposing your talent. I've done it myself several times, and it always paid off.

The goal of casting directors is to comprise a list of entirely responsible, cooperative, reliable, and talented actors. If you're not on that list, enrolling in one of their classes is a completely legitimate way to get on it. But first, check out their credentials on the IMDB to see whether they really are casting directors, and to gauge the level of project with which they are usually affiliated.

Also, many casting directors have a good eye. They can be very helpful with their observations. They can polish, and sometimes polish brilliantly. They can also simulate precisely the conditions of auditioning as nobody else, as that is what they do for a living. The neophyte actor can then acquaint himself with the audition procedure. Again, they can tell you what they like—and what they don't like—and that alone has a value.

I'll just end this by saying that casting directors can polish a Ferrari, but they can't build one. Ferraris are first born, and then disassembled, reassembled, and road tested at places such as the Actor's Studio.

However, not only can a casting director polish up the Ferrari, he can also bring it to a sale—something the Actor's Studio can't do.

"THE MAN THAT WAITS FOR A ROAST DUCK TO FLY IN HIS MOUTH WAITS A LONG TIME."
—Confucius

I love that saying by Confucius. Don't be a coffee shop genius. Don't sit around coffee shops waiting for your agent to make you a star. Once again, it is the actor's responsibility to prove to the industry what it is that he has to offer. The actor cannot rely on his agent. That's a mistake.

The fastest and surest way to develop, hone, and expose your talent to the industry is theatre. The actor is on stage two hours a night. That's a workout. Most actors, if they are acquiring the bulk of their experience by doing scenes in a workshop, are lucky if they are on stage a total of two hours in six months.

Then if the actor stays true to the principles of organic acting and doesn't whore himself out by crassly playing to the audience, he should develop rapidly. It's easy to get pulled off the mark when doing a play, though. Actors will soon learn where the laughs are, and then begin punching those lines. I guess if it's a comedy, perhaps some of that is okay.

Usually when a play opens to the public some of the actors in the play are represented by agents. If another cast member's agent attends, and you meet that agent afterwards, (with the represented actor's permission) it is not out of line to contact the agent later in the week for representation. After all, the agent has seen you in the play, so he probably has an idea of what your assets are.

It's also a good sign that the agent showed up at the play at all. Most will not attend—although they will fervently deny it. The agent who takes an interest in his client in this manner is usually an agent whose heart is in the right place. They're out there, but they're not easy to find. Even agents will admit that.

Craig's List has become a favorite for people who are getting started in acting. Because of the rapid technological advancements in video filmmaking, people are putting together short films for little or no money to display their talents.

Very often beginning actors will work for free to gain experience and footage for a professional reel. This is okay, but always have the producers guarantee you in writing these three things:

(1) **Your character must have a name.** If you do a part and your character's name is "Man standing next to a fire hydrant," or "Third girl with an umbrella," then that could easily wind up on the Internet Movie Data Base—for life! You'll look like an extra. The time may come when you are up for a major part. The producers check

the IMDB to scan your credits so they'll know what they can get away with paying you. Once they see a string of credits like the aforementioned then they'll offer you nothing—thinking that you're an extra who would be all too happy to work for their project for very little. Again, your character must always have a name.

(2) If you are offered a part in a film and are expected to work for free, then make sure you tell the producers that you are doing this film to build your reel, and that **you must be guaranteed close-ups.** Without close-ups it could be anybody up there. If they are shooting at some distance, and there are several other actors in the shot, then the footage to enhance your reel is essentially non-existent. At the time that you accept the part, simply tell the producers what you want out of working on this project—close-ups for your reel.

(3) **Have the producers guarantee you a copy so that you can transfer the data to your reel.**
Once you have footage for your reel, edit it in a way that is explosive and fast moving. Over your close-up should be the name of the film, starring (your name) as "Johnny Cougarbait," or whatever your character's name is.

Casting a film is a lot of hard work, and the submissions on major films are so vast that they are sometimes brought into the casting director's office on a forklift. The casting director will have piles of DVDs to look through. There is never enough time, so in many cases the casting director will look at the first twenty seconds, and then pop in another one. This continues until she has made her list for the director to audition.

If your acting reel slowly fades up your name, then slowly fades out, then slowly fades up a scene, then slowly fades out, you have lost the footrace.

When you have it edited, keep in mind that the casting director's hand, because of a chronic affliction called *schedule-cramp*, is always moving toward the eject button. But if it's explosive and fast-moving, cutting from close-up to close-up, from production to production, they will give it more time. If yours is edited properly, it gives the production personnel an avalanche of information in a short period of time—and that's good. That's what your reel is supposed to do.

DON'T BE DISCOURAGED BY CRANIAL DWARFISM

WHEN I first did scenes at the Actor's Studio several members approached me and asked me who I was represented by. I told them that I had just gotten into town and didn't have an agent. One very well-known actor said "I'm calling my agent and setting you up with an appointment today."

The result was absolutely one of the most unpleasant experiences I've ever had.

I was appreciative that someone would generously take the time to do this for me. I went to see this agent, a man named C. Rumor.

The receptionist sent me in to meet Mr. Rumor. His voice was, and I say this with no hesitation whatsoever, artificially sweetened to such a point that it staggered me. I had never heard such a saccharine voice in all my life. I could see right away that he was a man who wished to be thought of as "deeply caring and sensitive." He opened by saying that he had heard wonderful things about me from people at the Actor's Studio, but then he broke off, stood from his chair, and walked to the window where he looked out over the city, his face sagging with a tragic, melancholy expression. He then turned to me, looking twenty years older than just seconds before, and said these words, which I shall never forget:

"As I sit here looking at you I just have absolutely no idea what part—or what kind of character you could ever play." He shook his head. "I have no idea why people keep sending ... well, anyway ... I don't know ... I just don't know why people keep doing this to me ... it's not fair ...."

I said, "You mean you can't see me as a cop, a pool hustler, a boxer, a bank robber, an astronaut, a cowboy—or any of those?"

He started shaking his head again, and in an absolutely phony, syrupy way, he began apologizing. "I'm sorry ... don't be upset with me ... but maybe you shouldn't think about acting. Maybe you should think about camera work, or something behind the camera." We shook hands and I left.

Within a short time after that meeting I had played a cop, a boxer, a bank robber, an astronaut, and a cowboy.

Three years later I was walking down Sunset Boulevard when Rumor spotted me from an outdoor cafe, ran into screeching traffic with his tie flying in the wind, and came running breathlessly toward me with a wide smile and his hand stretched out.

"Jesse Vint ... hey Jesse, it's me, C. Rumor. How are you, man?" He stuck out his hand again, which I didn't take. He then grabbed my hand at my side and began shaking it. I stared at my contaminated hand during these following words:

"Jesse, I have been tracking your career, and wow man, way to go! I always knew that you had that special something, and, well why don't you join me across the street for coffee? I'm having coffee with an actress—a *real* blonde (he winked) from Amsterdam—so you might want to just say hello ...." He nodded in her direction and sure enough there was a young bright-faced acting hopeful sitting there looking in our direction, and not yet realizing that she was not so much a part of the business, but more like a part of the menu.

It went on like this for a very long five more seconds before I turned and walked away. I had to get out of there immediately to avoid a stiff prison sentence.

I've since learned that these experiences are not unique to the film business. An experience similar to this has happened to just about everybody at some point. Here's why: The film business is absolutely chocked full of moral dwarfs who use the business as nothing more than a way to get a girlfriend. They're everywhere. How? How? How do such people get their jobs—and keep them?

To get these jobs—

What forms did they fill out?

What lines did they stand in?

What courses did they take in college?

Did they audition against hundreds (sometimes thousands) of others for their jobs—as actors do?

Definitely not. Absolutely not. Not a chance. There are the good agents, who readily assist actors with their careers, and then there are the Rumors of the business; but whoever they are, they definitely did not endure the competitive gauntlet that actors endure. For the most part it's nepotism, family connections, friends, and classmates from school. It is the biggest single flaw in the business. Nobody knows how these people arrive in positions where they are making judgment calls on the most important information source the world has. The film business represents the eyes and ears of the world, so how do the Rumors attain so much power—and bypass the enormous wealth of competitive first-rate talent that is out there in this great country of ours?

Ultimately I am telling you not to be discouraged in the least by the Rumors of the business. You will, in your journey, meet at least one Rumor. But for every Rumor there are many truly gifted and fascinating people that will enrich your life tremendously.

Along this same line I'd like to mention:

A MODEST WORD ABOUT FILM CRITICS

FILM critics are consumer reporters. Some of them don't understand that. There are good film critics, who will enlighten the viewing public on the quality and content of movies playing in the neighborhood, and then there are self-aggrandizing devils, who strut around like little gods, wielding an unearned and undeserved power over the creative members of the film industry. One such ho-dad is Kenneth Turan—a smug, incompetent who trashed the film *Titanic* and its writer/director/producer James Cameron.

Kenneth Turan wrote *three* articles about Cameron—each of them several pages long—describing in detail how incompetent of a filmmaker he was, saying that Cameron "should never get near a word processor"—and on and on. I was infuriated by this vicious campaign initiated by the coffee shop genius Turan, and wrote a short letter to the Los Angeles Times. Out of thousands of responses (according to them) they printed five. One of them was mine. Here it is:

> Turan, like most critics, is only a coffee-shop genius. They can't write, can't direct, can't act and can't produce, but they pretend to know all about it.

If a thousand Kenneth Turans were put on an island and told to write one screenplay as good as the *Titanic* script, within a picosecond they would chop down all the trees, build rafts and get the hell out of there, because all critics secretly know that when left to themselves they are mere eunuchs who freely give advice to parents on how to raise their children.

Sincerely, Jesse Lee Vint III

Think about this: If James Cameron had listened to Kenneth Turan, then *Avatar* would never have been made, and the world would have been denied seeing what is perhaps the greatest film that was ever made. Amazingly, after this shocking display of stupidity and incompetence by Kenneth Turan, twelve years later he still has his job as a film critic with the Los Angeles Times. How? How? How? I'm not sure that we'll ever know.

The point of telling you this is that no matter how good of an actor you become, in your journey you will be criticized by people that did not have to audition for their jobs—as you did. Even James Dean and Marlon Brando were slammed by incompetents of the New York Times.

James Dean was "re-reviewed" years later by the Times, after the world recognized the genius of Dean that the film critics of the New York Times failed to do.

So don't lose heart when you encounter cranial dwarfism in the form of terrible reviews or opinions in the film business. Just do what James Cameron, Marlon Brando, James Dean, Clint Eastwood, and all of the very best and most talented in the film business have always done—keep moving forward.

WHY ARE YOU GETTING PAID? (A Reminder)

AN actor's job is to provide the heart and soul to his character. To give it a pulse, make it breathe, bring it to life, and in the end to *activate his soul* in a manner consistent with the character. An actor's job is never to tell the story; that is the director's job.

A writer's job is to provide the story, dialogue, and characters, almost always in the form of a screenplay.

A director's job is to re-tell the story that was handed to him by the writer. He re-tells the writer's story with the camera, and the performances of the actors. He is a storyteller first and foremost. That's what the director gets paid for.

A producer's job is to find a screenplay that he thinks will make a good film, and then assemble the elements, including the director and lead actors, and most importantly, he must raise the money. Finally, a good producer will steer these creative elements toward a harmonious, meaningful whole.

THE WORLD'S MOST REWARDING BUSINESS

THE film business, I believe, has more adventure and interesting people in it than any other business in the world.

I have always said that if you are doing a script that you like, on a location that you like, with people that you like, you don't have die to get to heaven—because you're already there.

There is also a sense of immortality, as the film that you are working on captures a time, space, people and places that normally would fly past without a trace. There simply is no business like it. I feel strongly to this day that it was and is a great honor to have worked in the film business. I have made a few regretful decisions, but not many. All in all, it's been, and continues to be, a wonderful ride.

At the 2008 Academy Awards with Debra Jo Fondren.

FINI

Recommended reading and viewing:

1. ***The Kill Bill Diary*** by Oscar nominee and screen legend David Carradine is the best book ever written for people that are curious about life on the movie set. There is none better.
   His book ***Endless Highway*** is an outstanding chronicle of the adventures of a young man. It should be required reading for highschool and college students.
2. ***On Film Acting*** by Michael Caine
   This book, ironically, doesn't dwell much on how to act. What Michael Caine does do (better than anybody ever has) is stress the importance of a strong work ethic, and how to allocate your time on the set, how to rehearse, and so forth. It's a terrific book.
3. ***An Actor Prepares*** by Constantin Stanislavsky
   This book is the mother of all modern-day acting theory. It's a great book.
4. ***Brando on Brando*** He doesn't teach acting in this book, but it's still wonderful to read the words of the greatest actor who ever lived.
5. Order from Amazon a DVD copy of the film ***Julius Caesar*** and watch Brando, the revolutionary, turn acting upside down. Acting was never the same after this movie.
6. I have mentioned James Dean's name many times in this book, so taking a look at one of his films might not be a bad idea. I don't have a favorite. All three of his films are wonderful. In order of release they are: ***East of Eden, Rebel without a Cause*** and ***Giant***.

7. Order a copy of ***The Best Short Stories of Anton Chekhov*** and see for yourself the kind of work that inspired Stanislavsky and the Moscow Art Theatre to revolutionize theatre. Ernest Hemmingway once said, "All writers start out by imitating Anton Chekhov until they find their own style."
All of the above recommendations can be ordered from *Amazon*. It's by far the easiest and most trouble-free service that I've ever used.

Filmography

Sister Mary's Angel (2011)
    Pastor Henry

Saved (2011)
    General Meade

Glory Jesus (2011)
    Pastor Kruger

A-List (2006)
    Star

Operation Balikatan (2003)
    CIA Chief Spencer

The Killer Within Me (2003) (V)
    Detective Lindsay Perkins

When Eagles Strike (2003)
    Spencer

Monkey Love (2002)
    Les

"Beyond Belief: Fact or Fiction"
    Detective (1 episode, 2000) ... aka "Beyond Belief" - USA (short title) - Connie/Positive I.D./Trucker/Cook Out/The New House (2000) TV episode
    Detective

Dreamers (1999) (as Jesse Lee Vint)
    Carl

Deep Cover (1997) (as Jesse Lee Vint)
    Ray ... aka "Checkmate" - USA (TV title)

XXX's & OOO's (1994) (TV)
    George Randall

Deep Red (1994) (TV)
    Det. Rhodes

The Temp (1993)
    Larry

"The Young Riders"
    Cody Pierce (1 episode, 1992) - 'Til Death Do Us Part: Part 2 (1992) TV episode
    Cody Pierce

"Matlock"
    Tex (1 episode, 1992) - Mr. Awesome (1992) TV episode
    Tex

Merchants of War (1990)
    Frank Kane

I Come in Peace (1990)
    McMurphy ... aka "Dark Angel" - USA (original title)

Another Chance (1989)
    Kenneth Rosika

"One Life to Live" (1968) TV series
    Al Roberts (1986, 1987) (unknown episodes)

"The A-Team"
    Insane Wayne (1 episode, 1986) - Waiting for Insane Wayne (1986) TV episode
    Insane Wayne

"Trapper John, M.D."
    Ben Cassidy (1 episode, 1985) - A False Start (1985) TV episode
    Ben Cassidy

"Knight Rider"
    Hank Kagan (1 episode, 1985) - Buy Out (1985) TV episode
    Hank Kagan

"Cover Up"
    Willard (1 episode, 1985) - Murder Offshore (1985) TV episode
    Willard

Downstream (1984)
    Chief Owens ... aka "On the Line" - USA (original title)

"The Yellow Rose"
    Matt Colby (1 episode, 1984) - Land of the Free (1984) TV episode
    Matt Colby

Dempsey (1983) (TV)
    Bernie Dempsey

"T.J. Hooker"
    Ben Edwards (1 episode, 1982)   - Deadly Ambition (1982) TV episode
    Ben Edwards

"Hart to Hart"
    Turk (1 episode, 1982)   - Harts at High Noon (1982) TV episode
    Turk

Forbidden World (1982)
    Mike Colby

"Bret Maverick"
    Tulsa Jack (1 episode, 1982)   - The Not So Magnificent Six (1982) TV episode
    Tulsa Jack

"CHiPs"
    Daws (1 episode, 1981)   ... aka "CHiPs Patrol" - USA (syndication title)   - Vagabonds (1981) TV episode
    Daws

"Walking Tall"
    Ben (1 episode, 1981)   - The Protectors of the People (1981) TV episode
    Ben

Belle Starr (1980) (TV)
    Bob Dalton

"The Incredible Hulk"
    Tibby (1 episode, 1979)   - Jake (1979) TV episode
    Tibby

Most Deadly Passage (1979) (TV)
    Paramedic Nick Halverson

"Emergency!"
>   Paramedic Nick Halverson (2 episodes, 1978-1979) ... aka "Emergencia" - USA (Spanish title) ... aka "Emergency One" - USA (syndication title) - Medic I: Seattle - Most Deadly Passage (1979) TV episode - The Most Deadly Passage (1978) TV episode
>   Paramedic Nick Halverson

Hometown USA (1979) (as Jesse Vint III)
>   Motorcycle Leader

Fast Charlie... the Moonbeam Rider (1979)
>   Calvin Hawk

"Centennial"
>   Amos Calendar (6 episodes, 1978-1979) - The Scream of Eagles (1979) TV episode
>   Amos Calendar - The Winds of Fortune (1979) TV episode
>   Amos Calendar - The Crime (1979) TV episode
>   Amos Calendar - The Storm (1979) TV episode
>   Amos Calendar - The Shepherds (1978) TV episode
>   Amos Calendar (1 more)

Deathsport (1978)
>   Polna

Black Oak Conspiracy (1977)
>   Jingo Johnson

Bobbie Jo and the Outlaw (1976)
>   Slick Callahan

Bug (1975)
>   Tom Tacker

"S.W.A.T."
Dallas (1 episode, 1975)   - The Killing Ground (1975)
TV episode
Dallas

"Amy Prentiss"
Factory Supervisor (1 episode, 1974)   - Baptism of Fire
(1974) TV episode
Factory Supervisor

The Godchild (1974) (TV)
Loftus

Reflections of Murder (1974) (TV)
Cop on Freeway

Earthquake (1974)
Buck - Jody's Roomate

The Disappearance of Flight 412 (1974) (TV)
Scanner

"The Rookies"
Pete 'Wolf' Gray (1 episode, 1974)   - An Ugly Way to
Die (1974) TV episode
Pete 'Wolf' Gray

Macon County Line (1974)
Wayne Dixon

Chinatown (1974)
Farmer in the Valley

Welcome to Arrow Beach (1974)
    Hot Rod Driver ... aka "Tender Flesh" - Philippines (English title), USA (reissue title) ... aka "Cold Storage" - Canada (English title) (TV title) ... aka "And No-One Would Believe Her" - Belgium (English title) (video title)

"Cannon"
    Al Sparling / ... (2 episodes, 1972-1974) - Flashpoint (1974) TV episode
    Al Sparling - Bitter Legion (1972) TV episode
    Angel Mellhone

"Chopper One" (1 episode, 1974) - Pilot (1974) TV episode

The Death Squad (1974) (TV)
    Harmon

"The F.B.I."
    Johnny Nesbitt (2 episodes, 1971-1973) - The Exchange (1973) TV episode - The Natural (1971) TV episode
    Johnny Nesbitt

"Mission: Impossible"
    Zinc (1 episode, 1973) - Speed (1973) TV episode
    Zinc

Daddy's Deadly Darling (1972)
    Sheriff Dan Cole ... aka "Daddy's Girl" - USA (alternative title) ... aka "Pigs" - USA (recut version) ... aka "Roadside Torture Chamber" - USA (reissue title)

Silent Running (1972)
    Andy Wolf

"Nichols"
>Charlie Springer (1 episode, 1971) ... aka "James Garner" - Canada (English title) - Where Did Everybody Go? (1971) TV episode
>Charlie Springer

"The Bold Ones: The Lawyers"
>Officer Taylor (1 episode, 1971) - Hall of Justice (1971) TV episode
>Officer Taylor

"Owen Marshall: Counselor at Law"
>Joe Boysen (1 episode, 1971) - Shadow of a Name (1971) TV episode
>Joe Boysen

"Bonanza"
>Toby Harris (1 episode, 1971) ... aka "Ponderosa" - USA (rerun title) ... aka "Ride the Wind" - USA (recut version) - Terror at 2:00 (1971) TV episode
>Toby Harris

Little Big Man (1970) (as Jess Vint)
>Lieutenant

"The Bold Ones: The Senator"
>Pvt. Wilson (2 episodes, 1970) - A Continual Roar of Musketry: Part 2 (1970) TV episode (as Jess Vint)
>Pvt. Wilson - A Continual Roar of Musketry: Part 1 (1970) TV episode (as Jess Vint)
>Pvt. Wilson

WUSA (1970) (uncredited)
>Young Doctor

"CBS Playhouse"
>Buck (1 episode, 1969)   - Appalachian Autumn (1969)
>TV episode
>Buck

Writer:

Trapt! (2009) (completed) (story) (writer)
The Killer Within Me (2003) (V) (writer)
Another Chance (1989) (writer)
Hometown USA (1979) (writer)
Black Oak Conspiracy (1977) (writer)

Director:

Trapt! (2009) (completed)
The Killer Within Me (2003) (V)
Another Chance (1989)

Producer:

The Killer Within Me (2003) (V) (producer)
Hometown USA (1979) (producer)
Black Oak Conspiracy (1977) (producer)

Editor:

The Killer Within Me (2003) (V)

Casting Director:

The Killer Within Me (2003) (V)

Self:

"The AMC Project"
    Himself (1 episode, 2003)   - Malkovich's Mail (2003)
    TV episode
    Himself

Macon County Line: 25 Years Down the Road (2000) (V)
    Himself
Archive Footage:

Reel Horror (1985)
    Sheriff Dan Cole

Jesse Lee Vint III

www.jessevint.com

CPSIA information can be obtained
at www.ICGtesting.com
Printed in the USA
LVOW13s0250020218
565034LV00024B/912/P